Rescued: My Stories of Divine Intervention
by Emmanuel Ike
Copyright © 2016 Emmanuel Ike

ISBN 978-1-63360-031-7
For Worldwide Distribution
Printed in the U.S.A.

Urban Press
P.O. Box 8882
Pittsburgh, PA 15221-0882
412.646.2780

Dedication

I dedicate this book to my dear wife, Ugo (U.G.),
and to my children and grandchildren.

To my wife: God used you to make me what I am
today. God used you to rescue me in many ways.

To my children: thank you for your stamina to
bear with me as I have learned to be a father
and a friend.

To my grandchildren: Be strong and courageous,
do good and perform great exploits
for God's Kingdom.

Table of Contents

Foreword

Hello, my name is Joy Ike, and I am the daughter of Emmanuel and Grace Ike. I am a singer/songwriter, lover of art, and a child of God. I am the third of six Ike children, and I currently live in Philadelphia where I am pursuing my music career. You are holding in your hand my father's first book, *Rescued: My Stories of Divine Intervention*, and I know you are eager to read it. You may be surprised that I am eager to read it as well. While I have heard a number of my father's stories, there are still many that I have never heard...or at least that's what he has told me.

I grew up listening to tales of my father's early years: what his childhood was like, how he met my mother, and animated recollections of his time in the Biafran War. There is much, however, I don't know. And in many ways, I expect this book will explain the man he has become. I don't believe in dwelling on the past, but I know that understanding it often gives clarity to the present and future. If anything, I believe this book will do just that, answering many questions my siblings and I have asked over the years.

As children mature, it's natural to want to learn more about the monumental moments that have motivated our parents to raise us as they do. I know that my parent's upbringing, which included famine, war, family upheaval, and the daily burden of uncertainty, has undoubtedly contributed to who I am today.

If I were to characterize my early years, I would say they were straight and narrow. We had a lot of rules, plenty of do's and don'ts, and absolutely no maybes. There was no middle ground or gray area. My parents were raising African children in an American culture, and there was no rule book, except for the Bible and the cultural norms they brought with them from Nigeria.

I love America, but it was difficult growing up here. I was bullied in school because I was African, and we (my parents, my siblings, and I) didn't understand a lot of the cultural expectations. I didn't know any better as a kid, and my parents were coming from a completely different ecosystem of rules.

That was painful then, but now I have a better perspective, as do my parents. In time, dad and mom have loosened up a bit, the older children have all moved on, and now they are raising another generation of children (my two adopted brothers) at home.

In 2008, when I decided to leave my marketing job to pursue a career in music, my parents were understanding. It was right after my oldest brother, Blessing, passed away. Perhaps they thought I needed a break from my job and would return to a "normal" career path eventually. I mention this because I'm sure my father will go into great detail about this season of our lives and how it affected each of us so deeply and differently.

We had faith to the end that God would heal and restore Blessing, so we struggled for years, and our family dynamic changed greatly through that ordeal. Everyone was mourning in their own way, and we didn't really know how best to mend ourselves back together.

My mother handled it by going into her prayer closet. That was (and is) her safe space. She was and still is the glue that holds us all together; so when she was deep in mourning, we all felt it. Now, eight years later, she has come through the fire, stronger than ever.

My father struggled just as much as my mother, but didn't show it to the same degree. I believe he was trying to stay strong for the family. I know for sure that Blessing's death was a big blow for him and I'm sure you will know exactly how he handled the loss by the time you reach the end of this book.

My father will also spend much of this book talking about his relationship with Jesus. As a child, church was a fact. We knew where we would be on Sunday morning, Tuesday nights, and every other Saturday evening when we held African Christian Fellowship (ACF) meetings in our home. Dad was the founding member and president of the Pittsburgh chapter.

Church was top priority for our parents, with education coming in at a close second. If there was something, anything that had to do with going deeper in our faith and knowing God, my parents pursued it and brought us along. We were taught that in life, whether you have much or little, whether your load is heavy or light, whether your friends are many or few, as long as you have Jesus, you will be the richest individual both in life and in death. My siblings and I have witnessed this to be true in both my mother's and father's lives.

Through all of our trials and challenges as a family, I know my parents loved us and did their best. One day, I will take their place and be a parent myself, Lord willing. When I do, I will have a wealth of experiences and lessons to impart to my children from my parents' legacy. This book will contribute to that legacy, and I hope you are just as excited about reading it as I am. Enjoy!

Joy Ike
Philadelphia, PA
January 2016

Introduction

I am excited to tell my story in this book because I believe it is important for several reasons. First, it will serve as a tool for teachers and educators who are mentoring and encouraging others, especially those who work with the underserved populations across the globe. Second, this book will help people who are in a similar situation as mine to find hope that they can rise from the pit of discouragement and hopelessness to shine in the purpose for which they were created.

Third, this book will help my children and the generations after them to understand their roots so they know that their lives have a purpose and should not be wasted. Fourth, anyone who reads this book will understand that times of adversity create opportunities for promotion if they pause to connect or reconnect to their Creator as a means to help them comprehend their seasons in life. Finally, this book will help encourage you to know that there is a God who reigns over the affairs of people. He alone is able to make something out of nothing, as He has done with me.

As you read, you will discover that sometimes life is not fair. I hope the stories with the associated dangers, setbacks and victories will help you know that you can turn around the situations in your life for the better, regardless of what has happened to you or where you presently find yourself. If you are working in the mission field in any capacity, this book will equip you to help others face the challenging situations they encounter as you minister to and serve the poor in their condition. To my children and the generations to come I say this: Do not stop telling the stories contained in this book, or using them to encourage and motivate yourself and others you encounter as you face adversities in life.

My life has been a series of one detrimental situation after another. In each situation, however, I experienced a supernatural intervention of deliverance that promoted me to the next stage of life. From these life experiences, I discovered that I was born to win. I assumed that if I had not been destined to win, I would have either been stillborn or not even been conceived at all. Based on this assumption, I concluded that I was created to be an overcomer, a man destined to positively impact other people's lives.

The name of this book is *Rescued: My Stories of Divine Intervention*. When I reflect back on my life, these are the specific situations I found myself in and from which I was delivered or rescued by God's mighty hand:

1. Early childhood despair
2. Enslaved as a servant by a wicked master
3. The Nigerian-Biafran War
4. Escape from illiteracy
5. Periled by poverty
6. Relocation to a New World
7. Bereavement of our first-born son

8. Escape from debt
9. Near death from a serious head injury
10. Deliverance from sin and death

When I remember how I grew up, I shake my head in awe of God and His power to protect the poor and needy. It makes me think of one of my favorite verses from Psalm 34:6: "This poor man called, and the Lord heard him; he saved him out of all his troubles." The thought of my mother not being around haunted me for more than thirty years. People who knew me when I was growing up doubted I could make it to adulthood because of the way I was left without care and tender love.

With my elder brothers and sisters gone after mother's death, I was alone most of the time, and literally ate whatever looked like food to me. My father's friends gave me a nickname of "Aja Igwu Igwu" which when interpreted means "sand." They did this because I often took showers with dusty sand and took on the color of the sand. Sometimes I ate it because it tasted good to me. Today I have eaten of God's abundance in a country far from my own. Yet I have reconnected with Africa in another way and time, and I will tell you how I got there and the circumstances under which I returned.

In this book, I will tell those stories of how I survived in Nigeria, how I came to America, and what I did when I got here. As I have read and re-read the manuscript, I have laughed and cried, and been reminded of God's goodness again and again. At times, I may be a bit too detailed, but when I wrote, so many things flooded back to my memory.

I want to include it all because it all means something and all helps my story of how I was *Rescued*.

Emmanuel Ike
USA
January 2016

Chapter One
When it All Began

I was the last born of eight children in the town of Nnewi in the East Region, now the Anambra State of Nigeria. My mother Eunice gave birth to nine children but my immediate senior brother died prematurely. When I was two years old, my mother also died and I was deprived of her tender care and love during my childhood. From that point on, my difficulties in life began. My childhood and teenage life were almost wasted if it had not been for God's supernatural intervention. No one desired to train me or show me the right way to live. My father tried, but was not really there for me because he was at the farm most of the time. I was shuttled from one family setting to another because I made the people taking care of me miserable due to my constant crying, depression, discouragement and frequent hallucinations. My desire was to be with my mother, and no one was able to console me in my misery.

After my mother died, my discouraged dad became a drunkard and a chain smoker, not capable of taking care of me. He was a subsistence farmer who always worked on the farm, looking for the means to make a living and feed his children. While I had a father, I did not know him well or remember ever playing or having a light, joyful moment with him. As a result, I was not well nurtured while I was growing up. Most of the time, especially when not at the farm with father, I was on the street playing soccer, without shoes on rough and hard ground, and making trouble with other children. One thing I did well, however, was to help my father on the farm. I had to do that because if I did not, there would be no food for me. Also, I loved to plant seeds and see them grow. I had to help out, for it was never far from my mind that my mother was not there to take care of me if I did not.

I was told a story that after my mother died, everyone was gathered in a room weeping, wondering what was going to happen to her children, especially me, her two-year old boy. That morning, I passed by to the room where my mother was lying dead with a plate in my hand, crying from hunger, saying, "Mama, Mama, come and give me soup so I can eat, I am hungry." That scene instantly intensified the weeping of the people as they were reminded of my life situation that was ahead. I was too young to have any clue as to what was going on.

Shortly after my mother's death, my elder brothers and sisters left home. One left to serve an uncle. Ruth, my one senior sister, gave it her best to take care of me, but was often bored and discouraged with my constant crying. I vividly remember her leaving me in a corner to cry because she herself was also bereaved and discouraged. Many believe that young children do not remember things from their early years, but I remember well certain things that took place during those days, especially my crying and how difficult it was for people to take care of me.

Eventually my sister got married and I was left at home with my father, my immediate senior sister Lydia, and my fourth elder brother, Sunday. We grew up together under severe hardship, helping father to work the farm while attending elementary schools at different missionary establishments. Sometimes we went to school only after fetching water from a stream, which was about a ten-mile round trip from our home. We did that without breakfast. By the time school was over, we hardly had enough energy to walk home. School was about a five-mile round trip and we walked every day. Sometimes we had no school uniforms to look like the other students. On one occasion after school, my teacher made me perform physical exercise while I was naked because I did not have a physical exercise (PE) uniform.

I never wanted to go to school anyway, instead desiring to stay home and cry. In our own way, my siblings and I made life worth living by playing together and sometimes fighting with one another the way siblings do. Dad was a strict disciplinarian and made sure to give us due punishment for every misbehavior. Moreover, neighbors were always ready to tell on us and sometimes help discipline us because in Africa, it does require a village to raise a child. This helped set boundaries as to what we could or could not do.

Close relatives were confused about what to do with me, as I was sick with near-death experiences, especially from lack of medical care. Sometimes I had serious infections from wounds sustained while playing on rough and hard ground with no shoes. How could I have shoes when there was no money even to buy clothes for me at the age of nine? My dad tried his best to take care of my wounds with M & B tablets, and they helped a little. In a couple of instances, I passed worms from my system one way or another, but God loved, protected, and preserved me because He had a glorious future for me.

As I continued to grow up into a handsome teenaged boy, periodically I attracted the attention of some adults who wanted to help. God sent these helpers my way, especially during Christmas and Easter time to take care of me. Those times of help were short-lived, however, and I still found myself lonely, sad and hungry, as well as poorly educated.

My teenage years started with trouble when I ran away from home with the assistance of my elder sister, the second child of my father. This sister was widowed early in life and returned home shortly after the death of her husband. Upon her return, she found that my father had remarried. I was the only child at home, then often overworked trying to help my father. My other two younger siblings, Lydia and Sunday, had left home to live with my elder siblings. When my widowed sister, Emily, observed that life was hard for me living with my stepmother, she arranged for me to run away from home to live with my eldest brother who was not informed of my sister's arrangement. The arrangement was perfectly executed through a 3:00 AM departure. I do not know how my father did not catch us because he usually did not go to sleep till the wee hours of the night as he kept watch over the compound to make sure it was protected.

We walked about seven miles that morning and finally found a bus heading to the big city called Aba where my senior brother lived. Since this occurred at the time before cell phones, nobody really knew where I was until several months later. My father angrily looked for me for about a year and was finally told I was with my senior brother.

Life with my brother was not much better than with my father. He was jobless and we seldom had even one meal a day. He became disgusted and told me that he did not know what to do with me. At this time, I realized that running away from home was a bad idea. After some time, he arranged with my other brother, a banker who had chosen to live with my older sister because she was brilliant, to send me to serve a master who had a junkyard business so that I could at least learn a trade. This was the business that my father wanted me to learn in the first place, because it was a common trade in my hometown.

I agreed to go and serve the junkyard master because there was no other choice for me at that stage of my life. To be honest, I felt like a french fry that had fallen from the frying pan into the fire. My junkyard master was a wicked man, a drunkard, and a solicitor of prostitutes. Many times, I escaped death from his hand because he would come home at about 2:00 AM while I was fast asleep. He would knock at the door several times but I could barely hear him. When I finally heard him and opened the door, I was greeted with vicious slaps to my face, hard beatings, and merciless flogging with no one around to help me.

After the physical abuse, he would ask me to mix a cup of salt for him to drink to help him throw up the excess alcohol in his system. One early morning, he pursued me into the street while I was running for my life, and flogged me mercilessly with a whip called *koboko* in the Nigeria language. This whip was made out of a cow tail and the blows from it were unbearable to absorb. He could hardly give me money to buy food because he wasted what little he had on women, palm wine (alcohol), and eating in restaurants. He did not care about what I wore or ate.

As a result, I dressed ruggedly and looked like a homeless young man sometimes. I was so ashamed that I avoided my cousins whose parents were well-to-do. When I saw them from a distance, I would run and hide. I was more of a junkyard ragged boy than a cousin, dismantling cars from accidents in which people had often died. In some of the cars, I found plenty of blood, body parts and skin tissue, and the smell was unbearable. At some point, I even tried to drink alcohol to numb my emotional pain. I remembered my father's behavior after drinking palm wine, however, and did not want to be like him. After two years, I ran away from my junkyard master to go back to my brother, trying to convince him that living with the man did not work for me. This is the rescue that I mentioned in the Introduction, for I see now that God did indeed rescue me from this cruel taskmaster who could have easily killed or maimed me.

When I was reunited with my brother, I joined him in a make-shift dry cleaning business that specialized in selling used clothing imported from the United States and Europe. I refer to it as make-shift because the irons used to press clothes in this business were primitive and had to be heated in charcoal for about 30 to 45 minutes, then cleaned with sand before they could be used to iron clothes. This was a difficult and hot process, especially in the heat of Africa. As I began to grow in my ability to reflect and think, I thought often about my purpose in life. I began to realize the pain I caused my father when I ran away from home. The desire to make peace with him haunted me frequently.

One day, I made a trip to my hometown to see my father and apologize to him. When I arrived, my father was working on his farm crops. Like the prodigal son, I went straight to him, apologized for what I did, and pleaded for forgiveness. My father looked at me and said: "Are you done running?" I was speechless. He looked at me and said that he had no choice but to forgive me. That reaction restored my relationship with him instantly.

I went back home as often as I could to visit him, and we talked about the issues of life. I even slept in the same room with him. This encounter produced healing to some degree for my soul. Although this statement is not specifically related to my story, I pause to encourage every son or daughter who may have had a misunderstanding with a parent to make an honest effort to reconcile. This will help speed up healing to your soul and mind, and release blessings in your life. Think of it: God used your parents to bring you into existence, and specifically instructs you to obey them so that it might be well with you, as promised in the Bible: "Children, obey your parents in the Lord, for this is right. 'Honor your father and mother'—which is the first commandment with a promise— so that it may go well with you and that you may enjoy long life on the earth" (Ephesians 6:1-3).

After I made peace with my father, I went back to live with my eldest brother. This time he arranged for me to serve another master. My brothers did not believe I was intelligent enough to be educated, and that's why they sent me off again. This time, I had to learn a new trade in bicycle spare parts.

My bicycle spare parts master was a wise and kind man who educated me well in the trade. He loved farming also and was just like my father. As a result, we worked well together. He had two young children and two other servants, so it was to me like being part of a real family. We went to the farm together, ate together, and played together. His wife cared for me like a mother. When he saw that I was industrious, he put my giftedness to good use on the farm, and preferred me over the other two servants to run his business with full freedom.

He even allowed me to own a small business on the side, which was profitable enough for me to buy a bicycle. In those days, that was to me like buying a car. On weekends, I would ride out to join my new family on their farm. There was something, however, that his wife could not understand about me. I was often depressed and moody whenever I thought of my own mother. I would frequently hide in a corner by myself, musing and thinking about what life would have been like to have my own mother around. I had hidden my thoughts so well from my master's wife that at some point she was tired of asking what was wrong and left me alone.

I often got out of my depression by pretending that I now had a real family. After reconciling with my father and being part of this new family, I noticed that my healing had begun. All went well in this family until the Nigerian-Biafran War broke out and everyone fled to their respective home towns from the city (Aba) after it was invaded by Nigerian soldiers. My master's hometown was miles away from my hometown, and we were separated. I took my limousine (my bicycle) with me and enjoyed riding it for some time after that.

One day to my surprise, I found my loving master at the front door of my father's house. He had come to take my bicycle away from me. This was painful to me to bear. I gave it to him anyway and moved on with my life. So the first seven years of my teenage life, 1961 through 1967, were in my mind, wasted. Then the Nigerian-Biafran War erupted and changed many lives, including my own. Let's turn now to that story, which for me represented more wasted years, but also provided another opportunity for God to rescue me.

Chapter Two
Surviving the Civil War

To the best of my knowledge, some wars were fought in the world, excluding terror, to gain freedom from oppression. Such was my perception of the reason for the Nigeria-Biafra conflict. I got a better understanding of the war from the books I read after the war, in which writers give different accounts of what happened based on the writer's knowledge and perspective. My understanding was that it started as a political crisis, shifted to a military coup, then to a religious-tribal crisis, and finally became a full-fledged, religious-tribal-economic war. My intention here is not to give an account of the war, but to give a personal account of some of my experiences during the war. One thing I know well was that I was a young adult 19 years of age when I was conscripted to go to war, but was released because I was tiny in stature, probably due to malnutrition.

A few young men I loved dearly who had lived in my compound (a family of uncles and cousins), some of whom had just graduated from high school, were killed in the early phase of the war. More than 144,000 innocent souls from my tribe (Ibo tribe) were massacred in Northern Nigeria. These things were difficult for me to bear and caused me to join the young men and women (some of them quite brilliant), who had no hope, having already sacrificed their futures and their lives to fight for the freedom of the Ibo tribe.

Enthusiasm was high at the start of the war, but as the cities of the Eastern Region of Nigeria (then known as Biafra) were invaded by the Nigerian soldiers, life became difficult for the people of Biafra. Food was scarce and air raids were rampant in the market places, churches, villages and towns. These raids were carried out by the air force of major world powers and were frequent with little or no resistance. They occurred even on Sundays and at night time. This made life miserable. Ibos of all ages were being killed mercilessly, and those alive were hunger stricken to the point of death.

I was always running into the bushes with others to hide, as if the bush would have protected me from bombs and bullets. Hunger was the norm of the day, and we went into the bushes gathering anything that looked edible. Many children suffered severe malnutrition. I was devastated to learn that a beautiful young girl in my hometown named Bridget was killed by a bomb that was dropped inside a market place in the city of Umuahia while she was there fetching food for her family. Moreover, heavy artillery and machine guns could be heard coming a few miles away from my hometown, which was 15 miles away from the active battle front near Onitsha. It was difficult for me to sleep at night because of the sounds of war.

After Bridget's death, twelve young men from my village, including me, had decided we had enough. We volunteered to join the Biafran army as freedom fighters. We were trained in 1968 and released to serve at an active front near my hometown to dig bunkers, trenches and tunnels. This exposed us to true war experience. Sometimes while eating a handful of cornmeal that came from America, bullets would fly into our camps and wound many. We had no guns, uniforms or helmets and our lives were constantly at risk. We were afraid but determined to stay and see the end, even if it meant death. We were shuffled from one active front to another, and eventually were sent to the war front to attempt to regain a major city that had fallen into the hands of the Nigerian soldiers.

This effort was a joint operation with some commandos and was successful. We achieved our objective until we were stopped by the River Niger when it flooded its banks, which usually happened during the rainy season. At that time, we lived inside our canoes at higher elevations, and moved around using canoes. Living life as a soldier in canoes was difficult. Any and all attacks were stopped by both sides. Occasional sporadic gun shots and teasing by the Nigerian and Biafran soldiers sometimes erupted into machine gun rattling. I was an assistant machine gunner at this time.

One day, the shooting was intense because on the previous day we caused some damage to the enemy. As I was feeding the bullets during this exchange of gun fire, the gunner suddenly shouted, "My hand, my hand!" My head was next to his left hand where the bullet struck. God spared my life right there as we stopped shooting and carried the wounded away to safety. This was my first near death rescue at the war front. The bullet could have easily struck my head because it was less than six inches away from his hand.

We continued to live in canoes in this little Midwest Nigerian town without the ability to enter into battle or initiate one. Food was becoming difficult to find, but there were still some oranges that had not fallen down from their trees. We visited these trees often for life support in spite of the bullets that whistled over our heads. We resorted to eating anything else that ran in front of us or lived around us that looked able to sustain us. Of course, the River Niger was our running spring of water to drink.

One day, it was necessary for me to visit the Biafran Freedom Fighters headquarters. I had a commando friend with me, but we did not know how to make this journey, especially considering we had to navigate the swamps of the River Niger. We were determined, however, to go regardless of the risk. We took off in our canoe with two paddles. As we rowed, the water was making a loud noise. When the Nigerian soldiers saw our movement, they began to shoot at us, thinking we were coming for an attack.

We escaped the intense gunfire after a frantic push and made it to see the Biafran Military Police camp to let them know about our mission. We greeted them, dropped some oranges off for them, and moved in the opposite direction, which caused them to pursue us. This also attracted more gunfire from the Nigerian soldiers. When we noted the Military Police were coming near, we ducked inside a thick shrubbery above the water levels. We stayed there until there was no impending danger and continued our journey after that. After a whole day of following the sun, we were lost, going in a circle on the River Niger. Ultimately, we arrived at the exact same place where we had started our journey – not making one inch of progress.

There was no food or water to drink but the River Niger. At night, it was dark and dreary with an abundance of mosquitos, monkeys, crocodiles and snakes. If that wasn't bad enough, our canoe was leaking. Our legs were white in color from being in the water so long, and the water was getting higher inside the canoe. We had no choice but to remove the water with our hands. We were concerned about how to stabilize our leaking canoe so we could get some sleep and gain some strength to go on for another day.

The solution was to anchor our canoe in the middle of a tree near the monkeys, while crocodiles slapped the water with their tails and mosquitos feasted on our bodies. It was in this place that I cried out to God to save my life and rescue me because I did not want to die without anybody knowing what had happened to me. As part of this plea, I promised to serve Him all the days of my life. The next day, we rejoiced that we had survived the everglades during the midnight hours and that God heard my cry, though I did not know much of how to serve Him then.

There was another day ahead of being lost on

the River Niger, and I was the captain of the ship. The commando with me requested that I relinquish my captainship and allow him to direct while I rowed with my hand because I had lost my paddle. I agreed and determined to tear any thorny bush or shrubbery ahead of us with my hands to make our continuous movement possible. We exhausted all our remaining energy tirelessly moving upstream. We also did not have much of any clothing on our bodies during this two-day trip on the deep waters of the River Niger.

At about 4:00 PM, as the shadows indicated since we did not have a wrist watch, we heard a human voice and the sound of a fisherman's tiny canoe. When he saw us, he was afraid because it was not common for him to see such strange faces in that environment. We called on him to come so we could ask him for directions, but he quickly ran away. We looked at each other, and encouraged ourselves that it was good sign because we at least saw a man who was not a Nigerian soldier.

We continued to row upstream, exhausted but drinking from the River Niger as often as possible. About an hour later, we ran into another fisherman. This man was bold and stared at us suspiciously as he paddled close to us. He sailed close and asked, "Who are you and where are you from?" I responded that we were Biafran Freedom Fighters who were lost as we made our way from our headquarters. I asked if he could grant us favor and direct us to the camp. As God who answered my prayer during my cry would have it, we were right at the edge of the camp without a compass to direct us. This in itself was a miracle, and I realized again that God loved me, rescued me, and had a purpose for my life.

The fisherman asked us to follow him to a huge Iroko tree. We obeyed but were cautious, watching to see if he may come with a knife to kill us. We waited patiently for him until he returned with a plantain porridge prepared by his wife to feed us. After feeding us, we drank from the River Niger again and gained much strength. He asked us to leave the canoe and follow him by swimming and holding onto shrubberies and trees as much as we could. We followed him, all the while afraid of drowning because the waters were at our neck level while swimming. At some point, he said to us, "This is the farthest I can lead you. Hold on the shrubberies, keep your head up, and go right toward the house ahead of you."

Houses in the Midwest of Nigeria are built on high ground in anticipation of the flooding season. As we began to move upland, a young lady came out of the house to use the latrine. When she saw us, she was courageous and did not scream, but rather went back into the house to report that she had seen two men at the back of the house. Coincidentally, the Biafran Major of the military region was in this house with his bodyguards and military police. I was concerned but confident enough that since I was a Biafran Freedom Fighter he would not harm me, but I was not sure how he would treat my comrade who was a commando.

As a result, I told him to say he was also a Biafran Freedom Fighter and he did. After that, the commander let us go free and assigned the military police to take us to the Biafran Freedom Fighter headquarters. He instructed the military police to bring us back for punishment and redeployment if he found out we were not Biafran Freedom Fighters. I was confident that I would be welcomed at the Freedom Fighters camp because the captain there knew me well and one of my friends was his main bodyguard.

Upon arrival at the camp, I learned that the Captain and my friend had travelled to Biafra for a leave. The people at this camp did not know me at all and that complicated matters. The military police said to me, "You are not Biafran Freedom Fighters. Get back in my canoe and let's ride back to the commando camp." It took quite a bit of pleading to convince the military police to let us go, which he did after we gave him some small gift. I immediately requested that my commando friend leave the Freedom Fighters' camp and gave him some money to find his way, which he did the next day. I stayed at the camp until my Captain came back from Biafra.

After the Captain's return from leave, I was in the camp for a short time when news came that the Nigerian troops had attacked the front where I was deployed and that many, including the commanding captain, were killed. I lost eight of my friends during that attack, and the news was emotionally painful to me. Some were buried at the war front by the Nigerian soldiers.

At this time, the war was turning against the Biafrans. The Biafran Freedom Fighters, including me, were immediately shipped to Biafra to defend the city of Umuahia. After we crossed the River Niger, marching to a town to be transported to Umuahia, there was an announcement by our then Head of State, Major General Chukwuemeka Odumegwu Ojukwu, that the Nigerian-Biafran War had come to an end. Yet we were still subjected to air raids, making the roadways and houses difficult places to travel or hide. Several days later, the Nigerian forces were commanded to cease attacks by the then military head of state. I walked home, which was about 25 miles from where I was, after the announcement that the war had ended.

The Nigerian-Biafran War took millions of lives, and my life was in danger many times due to starvation, air raids, bullets and mortars, and terrifying ventures. Innocent children, women and men died prematurely and many were massacred and buried in mass graves. To have come out alive from these dangers without a scratch on my body demands a lifetime of thankfulness and a yielding of my life to God, because truly, "This poor man cried out, and the Lord heard him, and delivered him out of all his troubles" (Psalm 34:6). God had rescued me. I went home after the war to try and continue the life that I had before the war, which provided God even more chances to rescue me. Let me tell you next about the days immediately following the war.

Chapter Three

In Pursuit
of My Education

The war ended when I was 21 years of age. I thought at my age, after all my suffering through my jungle experiences and the war in general, that I would have a chance to enjoy my life. Yet God by His mercy and grace got a hold of me and began to teach me how to live a better life. The early days after the war were difficult for me and many others.

After the war, a cousin of mine was determined to go back to the city of Aba, which was deserted during the war. As risky as this journey was, many in the compound where I was living decided to follow him. We jumped into his Mercedes truck, and on we embarked on the four-hour journey. During the first two hours of the trip, the smell was horrible as we saw many dead bodies, skeletons and bones by the roadside – all casualties of the war.

We arrived at Aba and settled into our late uncle's house. We were hungry, but afraid to look for food because there were still some Nigerian soldiers in the city, and we were not sure if it was safe. Therefore, we limited our movements until we began to see more and more people returning to the city. We did whatever we could to get at least one scant meal a day. Banks began to reopen, and my banker brother went back to First Bank (then Standard Bank of Nigeria). Shortly afterwards, he was paid his monthly salary once again. He was kind to start helping many of us to start life again.

He gave me some money to once again start trading on bicycle spare parts. I was traveling from one city to another to buy and sell those parts. This was a difficult trade because I had to carry all the parts on my head or shoulders and they were quite heavy. As I began to make a little profit, I went to the main market and rented a shop where I had to dress up every morning and go to work. Yet I was not happy with life. I was getting more and more depressed, trying to figure out where what I was doing would lead me.

Next to my shop was the shop of a bright young man named Philip who had completed high school, but his parents could not afford to send him to the University that had reopened after the war. As we spent time together, I observed something special about Philip. He was a young man with a quiet spirit, decent, always reading books, and he spoke English very well. I admired him and always talked with him about life in general. At some point, I found out that Philip was a born again Christian. He took me to church in an attempt to get me converted. I went with him once but stopped. He informed me one evening that there was a commercial school available for the uneducated who could attend at night, and that definitely stirred my interest.

After one year, my business wasn't going anywhere. Phillip had a sharp mind and was almost always reading a book. By comparison, I had an elementary school mind after failing middle school, couldn't speak simple English and didn't read very well. Phillip began to mentor me. He encouraged me to look into the school, and suggested some courses for me to take when I inquired about how I could be educated.

I went to my banker brother and tried to convince him to give me money to go to commercial school. He gave me enough money for one year of night school, but to my greatest disappointment, my school career ended after one year because the money had run out. I recruited a tutor but had no money to pay the one I found. At one point, I collected enough money to retain my tutor for three months but was too dull to grasp his concepts. As a result, he told me that I was like a full-grown palm tree that was bent and could not be made straight again.

That hurt me deeply but I sucked it up and moved forward because I knew for certain that God was with me. As I began reaching out, I met people who were determined to become successful in life. I proceeded to sell everything I had in my shop so that I could pursue an education. I concluded then and there that if I didn't have schooling, nothing else made sense in my life. People thought I was kidding, but I sold everything I had, left the market and came home to stay so I could study and learn. I began to make new male and female friends who wanted an education as well, and they were a good influence in my life. Some of the females were interested in me for some other reasons, but my mind was made up for education, and I did not want anything to distract me at that point.

About this time, my cousin, who was a Catholic nun, found out how serious I was about education and gave me the equivalent of $45 to take the London GCE. That motivated and encouraged me so much! I found three other young men who were in the same situation as I and we studied together for the GCE. Three of us were determined to take and pass the test, the equivalent to the American GDE.

Each morning, we met in an empty hall with chalk and textbooks, which I borrowed from a friend's bookstore. Those textbooks were published by Oxford University near London. We studied English, commerce, economics, accounting, shorthand, religious knowledge and math. We studied so hard that we stayed up all night with the help of coffee. At one point, I had a near-death experience, but was saved by my friends who poured cold water on me and sang songs to keep my soul settled. God spared my life from death that night, exhibiting His power to rescue yet again.

I had little money for food or shelter. I had a blue lamp and a six-by-six cubicle where I slept, cooked my food and studied. In one corner was my bed, in the other corner was my stove, and on the third side was my wardrobe. I called that little cubicle my high school campus and would stay up well past midnight reading and learning what I could from those books.

The problem was, however, that I would be

reading without understanding what I was reading. I would read and read, but it was like I was beating my head against the wall. I was not understanding the English, math or whatever the subject matter was. I knew how to pray, however, and decided to do that while I was studying. At some point, I knelt down and told God that I knew He gave people wisdom to write the books, so I asked for wisdom to understand them. I had become a Christian at this point.

I would pray and then read the text again. One year, after I consistently fasted and prayed, it was like I had been struck by lightning! My eyes were opened and suddenly my brain was energized. I understood the things I had never been able to understand, and education became a sweet, enjoyable experience. That was how God began to train and equip me academically.

I came to the Lord in April of 1972 when I was 23 years old. When I attended the commercial school I mentioned earlier, I met a girl named Joy who was quite fond of me. We spent some time with each other and went to dances together. One day when Joy came to school, I went to touch her and she said not to touch her. I wondered what was wrong, and she said I had to go to church with her. Because I liked Joy a lot, I said I would go to church and find out what Joy was talking about.

Keep in mind that these were the days when James Brown, the American soul singer, was quite popular in my country. I loved James Brown and I could dress, scream and sound just like him. I was actually looking for a way to join a rock band, because I had a good voice. That's when the Lord captured me and said that wasn't His plan for my life. So I went to church with Joy and sat with my James Brown-style pants, shoes with high heels, and my Afro hair. I was the first one to go forward when the altar call was given. God touched me deeply that day, so I had to step out and receive the Lord in my heart. God used Joy, who is still alive, to bring me closer to Him. She is also the one who introduced me to my wife, Ugo, commonly known then as U.G.

I came to the Lord in 1972 and I experienced a dramatic conversion. When I came back to our compound (yard as it was then called), there were many people there who lived in apartments. Instead of them hearing me shout like James Brown, I shared the gospel with them. They all wondered if I was the same person who they had known as an aspiring soul singer! Yet I wasn't the same person; I was a new man in Christ.

The church Joy took me to was a Pentecostal church. I was on fire for the Lord, but the Christian life wasn't really all that smooth or easy going, because I was a young man and had no foundation. When Joy introduced me to my wife, we were in small groups together. Then Joy disappeared for reasons I cannot explain, and we lost touch with each other. Joy and I reconnected in 2010, and I was glad to be back in contact with someone who God had used in such a profound way in my life. She was married with children, who were getting ready to go to medical school in Ukraine. My wife and I visited her and her husband when we went back to Nigeria, and we helped sponsor her children to go to school.

In 1975, I passed six subjects in one sitting for the GCE; English, accounting, economics, commerce, religion, and math. I had studied math for only six months and had a low level pass in that subject. Passing the GCE qualified me to go anywhere in the world to pursue higher education. My academic pursuit now became an exciting journey filled with hope.

My life was so different from that point on. God opened my eyes to understand what education could do in my life, but there was no way I could anticipate all that was ahead. I was a new person and my mind was suddenly and miraculously capable of learning, I was eager to learn and grow in my academics and in the Lord, but I had such a long way to go. God was with me, however, and I was about to embark on a journey that I could never have imagined and never completed without His help. Let's turn to that part of my story next.

Chapter Four
No Money

During my childhood, I had a fear of God. Sometimes I would go and sit in a quiet place, look up to the heavens, think about God and wonder how the universe was made. There was never anyone around to teach me, even though my father was a God-fearing man. He never explained his relationship with the Lord to us that I can remember, but every Sunday he took us to church. He would read the Bible, but we never had a family devotion. We grew up watching him read the Bible, but not really knowing what it was all about. When I was older and went out to the big city where I stayed briefly at my uncle's house who was a Catholic, I tried the Catholic church for a while but never really embraced the Bible. There was no one around telling me how to serve God or how to accept Christ into my heart as my Lord and personal Savior.

There was a move of God in Nigeria in the early '70s through the Scripture Union. This was right after the Nigeria-Biafra, war when people were looking for new meaning to life, which caused a genuine revival in Nigeria. In that move of God, my wife met the Lord, the story of which she can tell better than I, but I didn't know her yet. In 1972, I became a Christian as I explained in the last chapter. Christianity was an altogether new life experience for me.

Pentecostal church service back then in Nigeria was pretty much the same for every service. We came, sang clapping our hands aggressively because there were no musical instruments, prayed vigorously, worshipped, and then we listened to two preached messages. One was an explanation and invitation to salvation before the main message was preached. There was no doubt that the move of God was mighty in the land. The day I came to the Lord, a pastor named Richard preached a message that was an introduction to the meaning of salvation. By the end of the preaching, I stood up and was the first one to go to the altar to accept the Lord as my personal Savior.

It was seven years from the end of the war until I came to America, and those seven years were difficult for me. I was a church man, however, was serious about my walk with Jesus, and lived a holy life. In fact, I cut off any relationship with a woman who had been in my life because I had a new lifestyle. I locked everyone out, so to speak. My priorities were Jesus and my education in that order. Everything else I considered a waste of time.

My main barrier to my education was that I was poor, didn't have money, and there was none to send me to school after my elementary education. I resorted to prayer and fasting to learn what to do next with my life when I was in my early 20's. Many people were living and having fun, but I had an understanding that God wanted to do something special in my life, something unique. For a man in his early twenties, my desire was remarkable when you consider where I started. I didn't know how, but I was determined to make it with God's help. My dream for higher education became even more intense. I began to hear about different degrees, like a Bachelor of Science, Masters, and Ph.D. I was disturbed because it took money to get these degrees and I knew I had none, but with faith I pressed on.

One night I had a dream in which I was in an airplane going to a country but I did not know which one. A few months later, some of my friends who had finished high school were getting ready to go to America. I heard a voice in my spirit say, "That's the country where I want you to go." I was excited but responded, "It costs about $3,000 a year to study in that country and I have no one there to help me. Who will pay for it? How about my passport and visa? Who will get them for me? I need my transcripts and a sponsor. Who will help me with these things? What about airfare?" I bombarded God with these questions, but He took care of them one by one. Let me tell you how.

First, my friend Benjamin said to me, "I know how to prepare a transcript you can use to apply for admission. Go to the place where you attended evening school, get some stationary and rent a typewriter. We can use your GCE result and prepare a transcript for you." I borrowed money from a friend, and obtained letterhead and a typewriter. Using my GCE results, we carved out a transcript.

He also instructed me to go to the Department of Education in Enugu where the names and addresses of colleges and universities abroad were kept in a library. I borrowed money and traveled to

Enugu and spent the night at my cousin's house. The next day, I went to the library and copied names of schools of interest to me. I filled out the forms and mailed the admission packages with fees to three schools, all with money I borrowed from friends. A month later, I got a letter of acceptance to attend Huntington College (now Huntington University) to study accounting and business administration. This in itself was a huge breakthrough and morale booster. I carried this admission letter everywhere I went with great joy and satisfaction. I knew nothing about Huntington or the state of Indiana.

Since I had no food to eat anyway, I took the opportunity to pray and fast. I told everyone to stay away because I had to find out what God wanted me to do with my life. I often locked my door for three days with no food or water. I would put a sign outside asking people to come back and see me after three days. Then I would be in my room singing and praying, sometimes crying to the Lord. I often sang the words to a song to God that stated, "While on others Thou art calling, do not pass me by." I did all this because there was no counselor for me. My dad was not there, nor was my mother, and some of my brothers and sisters never went to high school. Those who went to high school were not around to advise me. To this day, I'm the only university graduate in my family. God met me during those times of prayer and fasting. That's how he revealed to me who my wife was going to be. That's when He also gave me a vision of flying in an airplane, and going to a country I didn't know about.

God gave me many other visions during those intense times when I sought Him. At that time, I only had the equivalent of about $200 in the bank. He showed me that people would help me get my passport at no cost to me. In one dream, a man came to me and said, "Here is your passport." And two months later, I went to church and there was a man, we called him Brother Irondi, who was rich and had a beautiful wife. He understood the plight of the poor in the church and tried to help us. Sometimes he would take all of us to his house where his wife would feed us after church.

During one such visit, I was talking with my friends about my school admission that would allow me to go to America. This wealthy man overheard our discussion and asked what we were talking about. We said that I had an admission to go to America, but had no passport. He said not to worry about that; he would take care of the passport. Then two months later, just like the Lord showed me in my dream, that man came and delivered my passport. So at that point, I had an admission letter from Huntington College in Indiana, USA and my passport. The next thing I needed was all my school tuition of $3,000, which of course I didn't have.

The issue of raising this money to go to the U.S. haunted me so much that I lost quite a bit of weight over it. I resorted again to regular periods of fasting and prayer. I took a step of faith and approached all the people I knew for money, but to no avail. One of my senior brothers was doing well in business. When all else failed, I went to him to ask for favor. He refused and I went home with my hopes dashed. Three days later after praying and fasting, I went back to him because I did not know any other person to help me. This time he agreed to give me $1,300, which I wired to America for my tuition payment.

I also approached many in my local church for sponsorship. Some agreed but their friends encouraged them not to help me. One of them named Brother Nwokeji agreed to be my sponsor contrary to the advice he received about me. With papers he gave me, the receipt for the money I had deposited, my GCE and my transcript, I went to the American Embassy for a student visa. As I entered the Embassy compound, I saw a sign inside the building that said, "Discover a New World." This sign excited me most because I had seen some of America in the movies and it was a new world to me. Unfortunately, I was denied a visa because I had not deposited enough money. I was told by the Embassy official that I would be a public disgrace if a visa was granted to me. My hopes of going to a new world to study were dashed instantly. I did not give up, however, but instead went home and began my campaign to raise money again to make up what I lacked toward the $3,000.

I went back to my banker brother, but he refused to give further help beyond paying for my airfare. I had no choice but to go back to my business brother with whom I had been in business in the past, but he refused. I am grateful that his wife intervened and encouraged him to give me the money, saying that I was the first one in the family who would have a university education. He gave me extra money but still not enough, for I then had only $2,777. While I was preoccupied with school, there was another matter that I needed to attend to, and that was finding my wife. Before I finish telling the story of how I raised the rest of the money, let me tell you how I found my beloved wife.

Chapter Five
Getting Married

It was in 1972 that I met my wife in a church in the city of Aba. There were many beautiful women in my church, and some were interested in me, even though I was poor. U.G. was also poor, but must have had eight suitors who were interested in her. I could sense that she was a woman of great faith and integrity, so we met in the church just as friends. She had just gotten out of high school and also wanted to advance her education. As my desire to go to school grew, I developed a special interest in her.

She was in nursing school hundreds of miles away from me. We were separated and only exchanged letters as friends, but whenever she came back to the city where I lived, she would have one of her brothers deliver a message to let me know she was around. I would then go to spend some time with her and we would talk about life in general, read our Bibles and pray. She would cook because she knew I was poor and had no food, and then we would eat together. Around nine or ten o'clock at night, I would go home. That's how we spent our time together during her school vacation.

Her mother never liked it, of course, wondering who this guy was who was visiting every time her daughter was around. It was only a relationship of friendship and fellowship at first, but my interest in her began to develop. In 1974, I got insight from the Lord that she would be my wife, but my approach to her about that subject was all wrong. One night, instead of sitting apart from each other like we normally did, I asked her if I could come closer to her. I told her I had something to share with her. I could tell she was uneasy about it. I said to her that it was God's will that she should be my wife.

When I said that, she literally ran away from me and refused to come back home. She thought that I had ulterior motives and didn't want to come back to the house again that night. She actually sent scouts to find out if I was still there. After waiting for a long time, I went home upset. I declared I would never go to see that woman again, because I felt so belittled. She returned to school but when she came back the next vacation break, she sent one of her brothers again to let me know she was home. It was difficult for me to go back, but I summed up courage and went back to see her.

Even though I was still upset, I kept calm and asked her what had happened during my last visit. She told me she was not sure what my motives were. She revealed to me later after we got married that she tested me to see how I would handle unpleasant situations. In those days, there was another woman who was quite interested in me, who almost enticed me away from the Lord and pestered me to marry her. I had vowed after being friends with this lady that there would be no more women in my life until I met the one who was to be my wife. The problem was that I still felt U.G. was the one for me.

My wife-to-be sent me a message to call on

her again and eventually opened up and told me that if the Lord told me that I was to be her husband, He hadn't told her yet. She told me I would have to wait for her to pray and, if she didn't get any special revelation from Him, it wasn't going to happen. That was a bit discouraging to me and opened doors for another two-years of waiting, which meant I had to wait four years in total after I met her before she became my wife.

We kept on seeing one another and I could tell that she was fond of me. Even when she went to visit other suitors, she would ask me to come along to protect her. Then after two years, the Lord gave me a dream of how things would be. During that period the Lord began to reveal to me things concering the suitor who was most serious about her. The Lord showed me that if U. G. got married to that other man, he would eventually abandon her. In the dream, I saw a man who took her by the hand, crossed the street and then left her alone. I saw the color of the car the man was driving, his personality, his complexion and his resemblance to a brother who was part of our local church.

When U.G. came back home for vacation, I told her I saw her in a dream with a man who was a university graduate with a white 404 Peugeot, and I gave her an exact description of his looks and build from what the Lord showed me. I told her, "He is very serious about you, but if you marry him, he will abandon you." She was startled and sat there staring at me, saying that description was perfect. The man had the 404 Peugeot and the color was white, and he did look exactly like a certain brother in our local church.

In the meantime, there was another woman in my life, especially after U. G. had kept me waiting. Her name was Miriam and we had a wholesome friendship. We actually had known each other from elementary school, so my heart was divided and I was struggling even though I knew U.G was the Lord's given. I wouldn't have gone wrong no matter which of the two women I married, or so I thought. One day, however, Miriam, who was also a spiritual woman and a prophetess by giftedness, came to tell me the Lord told her that she was not to be my wife. She then told me she saw my wife in a dream and that she had a fair complexion and gave a perfect description of U. G. That was the end of me wanting to marry Miriam. That was also the year when the Lord showed U.G. that she was to be my wife. My struggles of wanting to get married were over and the adventure of marriage began.

I set aside the $200 I had in the bank for the dowry before I left for America, but that wasn't nearly enough. In our culture back then, you were supposed to marry someone from your own tribe and village, and my wife was not from my village. We were of the same tribe, but her village was far away from mine. In our tribe, her people were known as warriors who in the old days used to behead their enemies and then run around carrying those heads, dancing and celebrating. So my brothers reminded me that my people were also warriors who had won many tribal wars with all the deadly evil that go along with those wars. They were considered dangerous and stubborn people. These two tribes had never really got along historically.

Those things did not really matter nor dissuade us because we knew that in Christ we were new creatures and old things were passed away and all things had become new (see 2 Corinthians 5:17). At first, my brothers forbade me to go to her place to get a wife. I personally didn't care, because I knew U.G. was a born again Christian, and the Lord had shown me that she was to be my wife. That was all that mattered. My brothers still refused and it was a very painful predicament.

I had to appeal to my dad, who was still alive then. Thank God that after running away from home, I had gone back to restore my relationship with him years earlier. I went home and, as I entered the compound, I broke into great wailing and crying, and everyone came out to see what was wrong. I didn't say anything until I saw my dad. When I saw him, I told him that I had found a wife, but my brothers wouldn't let me marry her. I had come to seek his permission to get married to this woman. I told him what the Lord showed me, and that I was getting ready to go to America. I also informed him if they refused me permission to get married, I would do so in America.

My father looked at me, saw how serious I was, and he was compassionate. Of course, he also never wanted me to marry a foreigner. He told me to get ready and he would go with me for the traditional marriage negotiations. One of my brothers did eventually stand with me out of the five brothers that I had then. My senior brother made up the difference of what I needed for the dowry. Even some of my friends refused to go with me to my ceremony because they knew that I was poor. In fact, my pastor, who didn't believe in me – which is another story – told them not to go with me to this traditional marriage ceremony. I don't know why they were all so afraid to go. The Lord, my dad, my brother, and some family member accompanied me to this customary ceremony.

We went from my village in Nnewi to U. G's village in Ibere, about a five-hour trip. There we had a beautiful traditional gathering of both families. We call this event wine carrying and dowry negotiations in my tradition. That night while we negotiated, my wife wasn't allowed to come to any of the deliberations. The negotiations were carried out by the men and, when it was time, they called U.G. personally and asked her, "Will you go with this man to be his wife?" She responded, "Yes I will go." I can still picture her standing on the porch, in the front of the place where she was waiting to be called in.

That settled it all, and it was a moment of great celebration. There and then, we were pronounced husband and wife. The men agreed on the dowry and completed the celebration. Her people blessed her with the blessings of peace, riches and fruitfulness, and we went back to the city of Aba. My wife and I had only a short time to plan for my departure to the United States, and two weeks later I left. A year after, she joined me in Huntington, Indiana. I was able to work two jobs in America while I was in college. I don't know how I did it, but my passionate love for my wife drove me to work harder so I could be reunited with her. I made enough money to help bring her over because we missed each other.

As I said earlier, I deposited only $2,777 for my first year school fees, and I went to the American Embassy again with my sponsor. He told me not to worry, that he would take me by the hand to the Embassy to defend me. In those days, you didn't have to make an appointment to go to the American Embassy. Early in the morning I took a taxi and went to where my sponsor was and we both went to the Embassy. They called me when it was my time, and I was nervous and trembling. They interviewed me again and interviewed my sponsor. There was one last question they asked him. They said that every young man that goes to America never wants to come back and they wanted to know if he could provide assurance that I would come back to Nigeria after my education.

God gave him wisdom and he said that I had just been married and it would be an incentive for me to come back to Nigeria. When he said that, the man looked at him, looked at me, and took my passport from my quivering hands. When he gave it back to me, there was a visa in it to go to America. Now I had everything I needed to go to America, except pocket money. My wife who then was a nurse surrendered her full month of salary, which was about $200 as pocket money. My banker brother gave me $200, half of what he had promised, and my brethren in the church contributed money to make up the difference for my airfare. I purchased the ticket and got ready to go. Off to America I went on September 16, 1976. My departure to the United States was emotional between my wife and I. The timing after our traditional marriage was not perfect, but I had to go because school had started.

I was able to make the trip that years earlier had seemed so impossible. God had made a way not only for my education, but for me to marry U.G. I was still young and naïve, and I was about to travel thousands of miles to a land I did not know, where there was snow and racial problems, and where I did not know a single soul. I didn't care about any of that though. All I knew was where I had come from and that God was taking me someplace new to help accomplish my purpose in life. Let's turn our attention to that adventure, and you will read even more of how God rescued me in the New World where I was headed.

Chapter Six

Coming to America

All I can say is that coming to America in 1976 was the Lord's doing. I landed in America late at night, and was disappointed by what I saw, or perhaps I should say what I did not see. After watching all of the American movies that showed tall skyscrapers, I didn't see any. I was in the Ft. Wayne, Indiana Airport, where outside it was flat with no high rises. Right away, I was discouraged and badly wanted to go back to Africa. I didn't know anybody in the U.S., not even a single soul. I came by faith because I heard this country was a land of opportunity where one could work and pay his way through school. Though discouraged and at some point depressed, in January 1977 the dream of the job and school both became a reality.

During that four-month wait after I arrived, I went to factories looking for work, and every time they would deny me because I didn't have the legal papers that permitted me to have employment. At the Square D factory, however, there was a man with a good heart named Bob. He looked at me with sympathy and compassion, and said he would really like to help me, but if he did, he could get in trouble. I said I wouldn't report him and I would take whatever job he had available. I kept going back week after week for four months. One January morning when it was extremely cold, I trekked back to Square D, my ears were as dark as coal from frostbite. They were burning and hurting severely. A friend had given me an old coat that I used to wear, but it wasn't adequate for the Indiana winters.

I was crying out to God, begging for help. God heard my cry and that January Bob said he had a job for me, even though he didn't think I would be interested in it. It was a janitor's job to clean the factory while everyone was working. I took that job with great joy. Not everyone was happy I was there, of course. I remember going to take out the trash and hearing some of the women saying, "Here comes that African again." Most likely, I wasn't fully acclimated to American hygiene standards at that point, and to be honest, they may have been able to smell me coming.

I worked the janitor's job and started making money – $2.60 an hour, which was the minimum wage then. After six months, I remained the only black employee in the factory. Usually I was the first to clock out and run home, fearing for my life because of some of the stories I had heard of how they treated people of color in the area. It then dawned on me that I was going to need a thicker skin to survive in the culture of the New World.

I had that job for six months. I was trying to finish my degree in three years so I was doubling up on classes during the summer. In spite of all these difficulties I was going through, I got A grades in accounting courses because, back in Nigeria, I had studied up through advanced accounting. I was doing so well in my accounting classes that the professor was using my name as an example of good work most of the time. I struggled quite a bit with science classes because they were all new to me at college level. After a while, a Caucasian friend named Bill gave me a bike that I used to ride to and from work. This helped me tremendously, but the bike was stolen on the college campus shortly after it was given to me.

I had a bad experience living in Huntington, Indiana, a small University town of about 14,000 people then. Parents would see a black person walking down the street and would be calling their children to come and see a Nigger. Some would be crying out, "Nigger! Nigger! Nigger!" I was depressed to the point of being neurotic, because it was like I wasn't a human being. One night, I was riding my bike back from work after second shift, and a car stopped at midnight and someone yelled, "Nigger! Nigger! Go back to Africa!" I was scared for my life, so I rode my bike through the alleys in fear of him pursuing me in his car. When I got home, my heart was pumping very fast. I ran to my wife and told her what happened. We prayed that night, trusting God to keep us safe. This experience haunted me throughout my stay in Huntington. I wondered if I died or got hurt there, who would defend me? God was faithful, however, and protected my wife and I through the days we lived in the town.

After six months of being a janitor, I asked Bob if I could have a job that would give me a place to sit down and work independently to avoid the women in the factory who picked on me. He promised he would do his best to help me. Later, he promoted me to work at a machine that inserted screws in transformers. Machine operators were considered to be doing a good job at Square D when they worked at 75% of established standards, but I was working at about 200%. Because of that, my promotions kept on coming, and I was able to pay my school fees and rent comfortably. I was making $7.60 two years later after starting at $2.60. The factory also hired my wife when she arrived after seeing how productive I was, and we started planning for a family. That's enough about work though. Let me fill you in on how it was when I started school in September of 1976.

When I arrived in Indiana, school had already started and I had two weeks of classes to catch up on. The assistant dean of students was a good man, but he had issues with the African race. He took me down to the international students' dormitory. African students were placed into a separate dormitory, which was quite cold. When we found the room was cold, we turned up the thermostat. When the assistant dean found that out, he locked it at 64 degrees Fahrenheit. You have to know that I was used to the temperature being 80 to 90 degrees back home. I didn't understand that raising the thermostat meant increased heating costs. Therefore, we piled on sweaters we purchased from used clothes stores and wore winter coats and socks to keep us warm at night

My money was running out as I purchased books and paid school fees, and I didn't know anybody to help me get more money. This was before

I got the factory job. I was depressed most nights. I tried to make some friends to help me acclimate and register for the right classes, but the academic advisor in charge of my major registered me for a full load of second-year, difficult classes. Remember, I had no prior high school or college experience before this time. There I was taking 16 credit hours, some of which were management classes, and not just principles of management, but the intermediate classes.

I wasn't used to the way Americans spoke English, and one professor in particular was talking too fast for me to comprehend my course materials. I would look around and notice that I was the only black person in the classroom. The professor would announce we were having a quiz the next day, and I had no clue what was going on, since I missed two weeks and couldn't understand anything he was saying. Of course, my first quiz grade was an "F."

I went to my dorm and wept. I felt horrible and my money was running out. When I arrived, I had $2,777, and it seemed like so much. It was almost gone at this time. Then I had another test at one point and got a "D" grade. It was multiple choice, which I wasn't used to because I had never taken a test like that before. Typically, I had taken tests in essay format during which you wrote out what you understood about the course material based on the questions asked. For that class I ended up making a "C" by the end of the semester. I registered into accounting 101, which helped because I was used to accounting. I had at least a 2.5 GPA at the end of the semester. Many of the other classes, such as American and world history, I had never taken before, and their tests were all multiple-choice format.

That second semester, I worked full time and had a full load of classes. Somebody was able to correct my academic advisor who had made the mistake of putting me through some difficult classes. I was then registered for the principles classes, History 101 and so on. That second semester I ended up making a "B" and my academic GPA came up to about a 2.8. Some people who had good knowledge of what school was all about wondered what was wrong with me in that I still couldn't "get it." It was simply difficult for me to adjust to the American academic system. Then a year later, my wife came and I was able to be more relaxed and made my first "A" grade in a non-accounting class. My healing from academic failure had begun.

I registered for statistics but was quite intimidated by the subject matter. The professor who taught this class, Dr. Hale, was one of the best Caucasian professors I have ever had. He saw that I was struggling. I think he had been a missionary, at some point, so he was not afraid to take me by the hand and tell me I had the brain to successfully do the work. He said he believed in me and that he would make it happen for me. On Saturdays he would be in the classroom early in the morning, waiting for me so he could teach me statistics one-on-one. That continued week after week for about two months. Finally, I grasped the principles and was able to run with them. The lights suddenly came on and I was even able to teach other students in the class, even though I had only six months of math.

I was making progress in school and with our finances as well. I had hoped that our church life would provide relief from the pressure we were under, but that was not the case. God continued to rescue me from the pit of ignorance as I continued on through school. Let's move on to continue the story of my time in Indiana and Huntington College.

Chapter Seven

Earning College Degrees

I was attending a Church of the Nazarene when I first came to Indiana. I had hoped when I joined the church that it would be a positive experience after the trauma of school, but it was not. I was also discouraged by what I saw in church, because I saw a lot of hypocrisy in the churches of that small town.

I didn't realize my lack of hygiene at the time, such that I would sit in a church pew and everyone would get up and leave. Probably because I did not smell or look good or because I was the only black man in the church. Only God knows. There was a white family, the Coys, who believed in me, and they had a little boy named Paul. They saw me as a mission field for their family. On weekends, most of the students traveled home since they lived only a few minutes from campus. The Coys would come pick me up to spend time with them, feed me, and allow me some play time with Paul. Their young daughter would teach me how to play piano also. They were the people who introduced me to the Church of the Nazarene.

Every Sunday, the Coys would call or come to pick me up and I would tell them I didn't feel like going to church, because I was afraid to encounter more discrimination in the church – but I went with them again and again. I almost became an unbeliever over it all, but I held my faith because

I had made a commitment to my wife to serve God that I wanted to maintain. Thankfully, I held my commitment to her until she arrived, but church attendance continued to be a struggle.

As I mentioned previously, I had gotten the job at the factory to pay my school fees. After paying my fees for the semester, and buying my books and everything else I needed, my money was almost gone, which also sometimes fueled discouragement. I wrote letters to Nigeria asking my brothers to help me out, but no one ever replied to my letters. I was stranded because my school fees were accumulating, but the Huntington College administration was kind enough to let me continue attending school without paying. That also became a challenge, but I prayed to God for Him to make a way.

There was no Internet then, so talking to my wife was almost impossible. We would write many letters to each other, and I would put some money for her in the letter, which sometimes got lost. When my wife arrived, I made arrangements for our church wedding on October 22, 1977 at the Nazarene Church. We had performed our traditional Nigerian ceremony before I came to the States, at which time we were declared husband and wife. The church wedding was to fulfill all righteousness in the eyes of other people.

My wife and I worked second shift in the same factory. When the bell rang at 11:00 PM marking the end of the shift, we would clock out, go home and continue our struggle as a new couple with school, work and family planning. I also registered my wife for classes in the pre-med program, so we had two school fees to pay. Her presence helped me to improve my academic grades. I did quite well in business and religion classes, but science classes were a struggle. My academic performances at this time began to earn me financial aid, which helped to reduce my school fees.

At the end of my Bachelor's program, I had earned only two C grades. Everything else was an A or a B. How did that happen? I don't know. God supplied me with great wisdom and of course I was a very diligent student because I didn't play around when it came to my academic pursuits. I made sure my assignments were done and, if I didn't know how to do something, I would do what I had to do to find help. Of all subjects, accounting was the easiest for me because, before I left Nigeria, it looked like it was the only thing I knew how to do. I read accounting texts printed in London and solved accounting problems. I would stay up all night until I found a solution to any difficult problem. When I came to the U.S., that diligence and stamina pulled me through accounting classes with straight A's.

I tried to take some tests to be exempt from taking the accounting classes because I already knew the material, but the multiple-choice format would not allow me, so I had to stay in the classes. I graduated with a 3.2 GPA with all school fees paid in full, and after I graduated, I dropped out for one year to work in the factory to make money to go for my Master's degree. During that year, my wife was working, and we had two children by then, Blessing and Victor. I saved about $10,000 to pay for my master's program. Looking for admission was difficult because I needed to score well on the GMAT exam for graduate school admission. GMAT wasn't an easy thing for me to take, again because of the multiple-choice format.

Every time I took this test, it would defeat me, and I assumed I would never have the opportunity to get into a master's program. My wife, however, has always been a great encourager in my life. Every time I wanted to drop my pursuit, she would push me to take it again. After being defeated so many times, I was frustrated and truly gave up. Through prayer and faith, however, I still believed there was a school out there that would admit me regardless of my GMAT score.

I began applying to schools all over the United States, and each time they would write me a letter denying me admission because my GMAT score was so low. Finally, Cleveland State University admitted me because they took my GPA and balanced it with my GMAT score. They offered a new major at that time called Accounting and Financial Information Systems. This program required writing computer programs, and whatever compelled me to choose the major only God knows, because I was almost overwhelmed by the degree requirements.

It was in the early 1980's when accounting software was just starting to become popular. When I look at it now, I see how God was guiding me because I was able to combine technology and accounting at its earliest stages. God used that to help me get jobs and promotions in the future. Of 15 people who chose this major when I began graduate school, only six graduated and I was one of them. I was admitted at Cleveland State University in September 1981 and graduated in June 1983. While at Cleveland State, the Peachtree accounting software was introduced. QuickBooks hadn't even been in the market yet, and Lotus 1-2-3 was then the king of spreadsheets and was also brand new. Part of the Master's program was to go out and do research on how the accounting firms were using the new software to do their work.

My family did not move to Cleveland with me. They stayed back in Fort Wayne, Indiana while I lived near the campus in Cleveland. It was about a three-hour drive, and every weekend I would go home to spend time with my family. I would finish my computer lab training in COBOL, PASQAL and all the other advanced program languages as required in this major, and then jump in my car for the commute back to Fort Wayne. Early Monday morning, I would return to campus in Cleveland to once again take my classes.

One night during this commute, I almost lost my life. I left campus at 2:00 AM on Saturday morning to drive to Fort Wayne. Around 2:30 or 3:00 AM, I fell asleep at the wheel and there was a semi-truck coming down a two-way road. When I opened my eyes, I could see the truck's tires from what seemed like less than a foot away from me. I swung my car to the right, and my heart raced like never before, not even during my war experience. In fact, I should have been a dead man, but God rescued me by waking me up. I truly thank God for His mercy! I was reminded once again that God had a special purpose for me while I pulled over and got a few hours of sleep. That was the end of the late-night drives. If I worked too long into the night, I would catch some sleep and drive to Fort Wayne the next day.

In 1983, I graduated and my wife decided it was her turn to go to school. She attended Purdue University and earned her undergraduate degree in nursing, even though she was already a registered nurse in Nigeria before coming to the United States. She completed her bachelor's degree in nursing in 1985. Then it was a question of whether she would go into the school of pharmacy or medical school.

I told her she wasn't going anywhere and that we should calculate all the salaries and years of struggles that we had been through. I was thinking like a good accountant, and it was time to make some money. My argument was that we were headed for the same lifestyle of not having money and not having time together for the next seven years if she stayed in school. After we argued and fought about it for months, I had to yield to her desire for medical school because that's what she really wanted to do. That's how we ended up in Pittsburgh in 1987.

She was admitted to the University of Pittsburgh Medical School in 1987, after having four children, and graduated in 1991. This was a difficult time for our marriage and our friendship was seriously challenged. U.G.'s mother arrived from Nigeria to help raise the children, and stayed with us until the children were grown and graduated from college. While U.G. was in school, I had to work to support the family. Once again I was faced with tremendous challenges. I found God just as faithful as He had been in getting me through school.

Chapter Eight
Climbing the Corporate Ladder

I had landed a job back in Fort Wayne – even though for a long time I was an immigrant with no green card (legal residency in the U.S.). Finally, General Telephone, or GTE as it was called, determined that I was worthy of employment. I started there in 1985 through a temporary employment agency and worked there for about a year as a revenue accountant. Initially, this work was done manually with pencil and paper, but after about six months, Lotus 1-2-3 came out. GTE purchased IBM personal computers, and trained its accountants to use the software to do accounting.

Then after a year, a job opened up for me at the Fort Wayne Chamber of Commerce, which was looking for a full-time bookkeeper. A Christian young man by the name of Richard was the controller at this organization. He interviewed me and asked whether I had my citizenship or green card. My response was that it was in the making, He did not pursue that topic any further after my response, and still decided to take me in. He gave me a job as a bookkeeper (even though I had a Master's degree in accounting) at the Chamber. I did not hesitate to take the job because I wanted a chance to prove myself. This was in 1985.

Now I had an opportunity to manage an

entire organization's accounting system, my first real management experience. I took the position and turned that place around. It was proof that I could do the job, or at least that's what I told myself. In the same year, I went in to negotiate a title change and pay increase because I was merely listed and paid as a bookkeeper. I started the job with a salary of $17,000 and was being paid $18,000 annually after my last pay raise.

I argued that I had proven myself and had managed the projects assigned to me effectively. At that time, we had acquired accounting software and an IBM mainframe computer system to manage our finances, and I was able to master how it all worked. It was easier for external auditors to do their work after I had cleaned things up in house. I talked to my boss Richard about a pay increase and title change to an accountant but he said he talked to the president of the Chamber who refused. Richard suggested I go and ask the president myself. I summoned the courage to go and talk to him. He was a dynamic man, but before I talked to him, I had started sending my resumes out – just in case.

Two openings emerged from my search. One was at Lincoln Insurance and the other was at Mutual Security Life Insurance Company, which has since closed its doors. Mutual Life, as it was called, offered me a job with a significant pay increase. I had a letter offering employment, which gave me additional courage to talk to the Chamber president. But I loved working for the Chamber of Commerce and did not want to leave. During our discussion, the president refused my request, so I drafted and submitted my resignation. That was at the end of 1986.

I went to Mutual Life and was able to buy my first real car. At that point, I felt like I had made it in America and my life was beginning to change for the good. I worked as a mortgage loan accountant for three months at Mutual Life. When I first started, the department I was assigned to was in an accounting mess. I began to find problems and solutions for how things could be fixed and done properly. Anna, my supervisor, was a lovely lady and called the manager of internal audit who said she felt the company had an auditor in the house. That was four months after I accepted the job. The manager of the internal audit department by the name of Paul called me to go out and have lunch. I had no idea what was in the making. At lunch, he told me what Anna had said and invited me to come interview for an auditor position.

I had wanted to be an auditor since I was in college, but I didn't have the necessary legal papers. As a result, no one gave me a chance. Most of the people who graduated with me found jobs right after school. After the interview, I accepted the position as a staff auditor. After just four months, I transitioned from being a mortgage loan accoun tant to a staff auditor and was scheduled for a trip to Fresno, California for training.

By now, I had become a legal resident of the U.S. My wife had a nursing degree and it was easy in those days for nurses to obtain their green cards. She applied for my green card, but the immigration official rejected my application because I had worked in the factory while in school without legal papers. They said I would have to go outside America to get my green card. I couldn't go to Nigeria, because if I did, I would get stuck there because there were many on a waiting list for a green card in my home country.

Instead, I flew to Togo, a small country without as many educated people wanting to go to America as in Nigeria. When I came in for interview, they told me that by rights I should go and apply through Nigeria. Then they gave me a way out and told me that if I could prove that I was a Nigerian citizen, they would give me a visa. I immediately went to the Nigerian Embassy and told them why I was there and showed them my Nigerian passport as proof of my Nigerian citizenship. I found a man who didn't ask for a bribe, which was the norm in a situation like mine, who was able to write a letter of proof of Nigerian citizenship for me instantly.

The next morning, I took the letter to the American Embassy in Togo and pleaded with them to be quick, because my wife was expecting our third child (Joy) soon. God was with me, and surprisingly my visa came right back in less than a week. When I came back to the States, the other insurance company, Lincoln, offered me a job. I wasn't quite a year at Mutual and I was confused as to what to do, because Mutual was a good company and they needed minority accountants. The CEO at Mutual was a good man, and he advised that I should not take the new offer from Lincoln.

I turned in my resignation anyway, but Mutual matched the salary Lincoln had offered to pay me and promised me a promotion in the next year. I had already accepted the Lincoln position who was also looking for minority accountants. I was also making inroads toward my Certified Public Accouting (CPA) qualification after passing three of the four required sections. Not only did Lincoln offer me the job, they sent flowers to my wife at home and asked her to beg me to come work for them.

The Vice President of Finance at Lincoln invited me to his house for dinner because they wanted me quite badly. Therefore, I accepted and came back and told my boss at Mutual what I was going through, but he insisted that I wasn't going anywhere. Needless to say, I was quite disturbed about the whole situation. The position at Lincoln was for a mutual fund accountant and I wanted to learn more about mutual funds. They felt I had enough experience to be able to do the work.

I had to turn the Lincoln offer down in order to stay at Mutual, which was a medium-sized company that was family-oriented with a lot of Christians working there. In a sense, that was my mid-life crisis, trying to make that employment choice. I thought that was the end of it. A year later in 1987, my wife accepted admission to the University of Pittsburgh Medical School. Then it was my turn to find a way to move and join her and the children because, when she was admitted, she took everyone with her. I was alone in Fort Wayne.

Every weekend as I had done while getting my degree in Cleveland, I was traveling from Fort Wayne to Pittsburgh to see my family. This time, the distance was too great, so I informed my wife that I couldn't handle it any more, and started looking for a job in Pittsburgh. This is how I came to work at a Fortune 500 company located in downtown Pittsburgh. They offered me $33,000 a year as a mid-level auditor. I accepted it and moved, but someone warned me not to go to that company because he had heard the company never treated minorities well. I responded that my family was in Pittsburgh already, I had to move, and would use that job as a stepping stone to something else.

I accepted the position and, after five years, I realized the man's warning to me was true. It was a disaster. When I started with my professional life, a Caucasian man had advised me to move from one company to another every two years. He felt that was the only way educated minority people got promotions and pay raises. I didn't listen to him. I stayed for ten years at this Fortune 500 company, much too long.

My time there ended in a legal battle because they had promoted 19 people over me, some of whom I trained, giving them good positions in the company. I was passed over for a promotion every time these people were advanced. I had to fight them for my own raise and promotion, which only occurred twice. Then at one point, they promoted someone who was in a junior staff position years after I was employed to be my supervisor. They instructed me to take her into the field to teach her environmental auditing, but I refused. Then the legal battle began.

While making inquiries into my personal files, I found out that my audit manager had investigated me for travel expense statement abuse. I had lived for six years in Pittsburgh, and for three years of that I was in the air traveling someplace for the company conducting audits. When difficult jobs would come, I would be called on, indicating that they had confidence that I was doing a good job. Several times my supervisor called me into his office to tell me I was doing an excellent job. Each time he recommended me for a promotion, the company would turn him down.

I went and pulled the personnel files from my departments of all the names of the people recruited from college whom I trained. In each case, when good positions came open, the company would give it to others, the majority of whom were Caucasians. The only way I found out was when the company gave me an unexpected raise. At one point I was performing an audit at one of the company's plants and suddenly, in the middle of the year when they usually do not give raises, the company called and said they believed I was doing a fine job, and that they were going to give me a 7% raise again, as they had the year before. I noted this was their usual pattern of giving me a raise whenever they were ready to promote someone over me. The standard raise with a promotion, however, was 10% with a change of title.

At that point, I said that was the end of it with the company, and I looked for a lawyer to advance my cause and protect me from their anticipated counterattack. I won my case of discrimination, and my lawyer said I had a very good case, and asked me if I wanted to take my case to court or settle. For a number of reasons, I chose to settle. In a sense, that represented another rescue, for God intervened on my behalf and rescued me from mean-spirited discrimination of a major corporation.

In 1997, after I had left that Pittsburgh company, I joined a consulting firm established by a Nigerian business lawyer who hired me as vice president of consulting. He matched my Fortune 500 company's salary of $50,000. We were consulting with the State of Pennsylvania, local counties and small businesses. I joined this company, but that position didn't last long because I really wanted to be in public accounting.

Then I met a Christian accountant who was expanding his firm and he invited me in as a partner in his firm with an offer of 20% ownership. That was a big shift from being in consulting to the public accounting world. I stayed there for four years, designing accounting systems and training people to run them. After four years in 2003, I had to form my own firm called Accounting and Consulting Solutions, Inc., which is now named Precept Consulting, Inc.

The reason I made that transition was because the public accounting practice of designing an accounting system and auditing the same system was stopped by the U. S. Accounting Standard Board after Enron and many other entities collapsed. That is how I ended up in the consulting world. I left to start my company with four clients from the public accounting firm and within a year, I was able to build my firm up to thirteen clients. I was also able to increase my revenues above what I was generating in the public accounting world, and maintained much better relationships with my clients.

At the time of the infamous scandal and collapse of the Enron Corporation, I had had enough of America and employment. I needed to be on my own, which is typical thinking for people from my tribe, for we love to own our own businesses. I opened my firm in 2004 and it went well until the economic meltdown in 2008. I stayed in business until 2011, when I began to struggle. I desperately tried to stay in business so I could raise my family here and help my family back in Africa, and in doing so I incurred a large amount of debt to keep the doors open.

Before I knew it, I had $80,000 in debt. I agonized in my spirit because I considered America to be my Promised Land. I knew where God brought me from, and He didn't bring me to the U.S. for me to fail. I was confident God would get me out of debt, but I didn't know how. I prayed that just how the Lord helped the children of Israel to enter into the Promised Land, He would do for me. I reassured myself that God was with me, and would never leave or forsake me. I also encouraged myself with this verse from Paul's hand: "I am confident of this, that He who began a good work in me will complete it until the day of the Lord Jesus Christ" (Philippians 1:6).

After the death of my son (more on that later) in 2008, I moved my office into my home because I had a handful of people who were struggling to pay me. Some of them owed me thousands of dollars and still do to this day. Clients weren't paying and I was telling God that I was here, needed money to feed my family and run my business, and He needed to do something for me. One day in May of 2011, I finished praying and fell asleep, while agonizing in my spirit.

While I was sleeping, the Lord lifted up the entire room and took me to the back of my house. There I saw a rectangular flood area over which I was flying in the spirit. It looked like the flood was ready to swallow me, but God would not allow me to sink. He had me floating over and around, up and down. I believe I was half awake and half asleep.

When I woke up, I asked God what kind of vision this was and requested an interpretation. About two weeks later, I heard a whisper in my spirit to call a friend of mine named Audrey Murrell, who was a professor of business at the University of Pittsburgh. I met Audrey when she was the treasurer for a church I had helped by restructuring their financial accountability. The church had no idea where they stood financially, even though they had been in existence for years. Audrey retained me as a consultant to help turn around the financial reporting at the church, which I did.

I helped the church identify their assets, revamp their contributions reporting, prepared the first financial statements, and designed an accounting system. I also trained Audrey to run the system. After it was all said and done, I received an ovation along with a gift from the Church board. From that point on, Audrey was able to present financial statements to the church, and their contributions increased from that point forward. Audrey has never forgotten me since then.

In June 2011, Audrey was the chairperson of the board for the Northside Christian Health Center and called me to become the treasurer of the organization to help revamp financial reporting. I could not continue long as the treasurer of this Center because I was also working on my doctoral degree (more on this later). After my dream, I heard a whisper in my spirit to call Audrey and find out how the Center was doing. Audrey called me three days later and asked me to come in and help the Center out because the CFO was no longer with the organization. The executive director was glad to hear from me, and I was willing to go back to help. I began with this organization as a consultant but was aware the opportunity was there for me to become the next CFO of the Center.

I struggled with that thought of being an employee again because, as you remember, I had vowed not to work for anyone else after my bad work experience in corporate Pittsburgh. As I was considering the CFO position, a minister was lodging at my house and he told me to go visit the Center and he would pray for me. I met with the director, who informed me that he was paying large fees for financial consulting. During the meeting at which Audrey was also present, I reluctantly said that if this position was available, I would consider it. This immediately triggered an offer for me to take the CFO job. By the time I got home, my contract was in my email. The offer was attractive and sufficient to replace my consulting revenues I had received when the American economy was thriving. I was also allowed to continue with my consulting work as time permitted.

Even in the midst of a bad economic downturn, God made a way for me. I was able to solve the organization's accountability and compliance problems. I got paid well enough to pay back the $80,000 I owed and was debt free – that is how God rescued me from my indebtedness. God's economy is a transcendent economy that allows Him to do anything any time He pleases, regardless of how the world's economy is functioning. God answered my prayer in that I didn't want to leave this Promised Land (America) empty handed. I didn't know how He would bring me out of debt, but He did. "Thanks be to God who always leads us in triumph in Christ, and diffuses the fragrance of His knowledge in every place" (2 Corinthians 2:14).

I have shared with you this story of financial victory, but in the next chapter I will tell you a not-so-happy story of the loss of one of our children to sickness. It is not an easy story to tell, and I have wept as I wrote and re-read the words that bring back all the pain and sorrow of that sad event. I will give you just some of the highlights as the full story may be enough to fill a separate book. Let's go there now.

Chapter Nine
The Death of Our First Born

My wife and I were doing well after all the struggles early in our lives and marriage. The children had all graduated from college and gone to live on their own, but the enemy wasn't really happy with us. We loved our children and were financially blessed to some degree. Blessing, our oldest son, was the first to graduate from high school. During his first year at Clarion University, he had a poor GPA and dropped out of school at one point. At that time, we brought him home to attend the community college to see if he could regroup his life, which he did. He earned a good GPA and we felt it was time for him to go back out to Clarion and graduate. He received some scholarship funds and graduated as an elementary school teacher.

He got a position in the Baltimore, Maryland school district and taught there for one semester. After that semester, Blessing was diagnosed with Hodgkin's lymphoma. We decided that he should come home for treatment, because we felt like Pittsburgh was a better place for us to take care of him. In early 2004, Blessing returned home and began treatment at Mercy Hospital in Pittsburgh. I had just started my business in January 2014 and didn't have time to launch it as I desired, but that didn't discourage me. We kept on taking care of Blessing, and believed that after six months he would recover.

First, they did a bone marrow test to determine if the cancer had spread, but there was no evidence that it had. They inserted a port on his chest so he could receive chemotherapy. His doctor was getting ready to go to Israel, and my wife, who is also a physician, suggested that they disconnect the port and reconnect it when the doctor got back from vacation after a few weeks. The doctor did not agree and insisted that the port remain intact until his return. That decision would have serious implications as we were to discover.

In the meantime, Blessing was having great fun with children at the YMCA Camp Kon-O-Kwee where he worked. So he went back to Camp Kon-O-Kwee with a port on his chest, playing around with children. In the process, the port entry got infected to the point where the tube inserted for the port dropped out. Blessing was a man who was strong in spirit and felt like he could survive anything. He carried the port around with him and didn't pay much attention until he developed a high fever.

At some point, however, it was so bad that he rushed himself to the emergency room. We almost never check the voicemails on our house phone, but woke up early one morning and as my wife was going out the door, she had a flash of woman's intuition, which is usually spot on. She checked the phone, saw there was a voicemail, and listened to a message from a hospital to let us know that Blessing was in the emergency room in a hospital near Zelienople, Pennsylvania.

After that, Blessing was rushed to Mercy Hospital in an ambulance, and that was the end of the treatment for cancer because the infection had to be treated first. When he was in the hospital, he got a hospital infection, which worsened the situation. This lasted more than a month while the cancer was spreading. The doctors were fighting an infection that was stubborn and refused to subside.

By the time they got the infection under control, the cancer was everywhere in his body. The hospital began chemotherapy and many types of it, but none of them produced a positive result. At some point, they even did a bone marrow transplant. The morning they were to do the transplant, the marrow they harvested got infected again. They decided to proceed in spite of the infection, but it didn't produce any good results. That's when my wife told them to stop the chemotherapy so we could try some alternative medicine. My wife continued Blessing's treatment using several kinds of alternative medicines that kept him going for years. All those years, we mobilized prayer for him everywhere possible. At one point, Blessing was always on oxygen and carried it everywhere he went.

Later in treatment, he went into a coma for four days and wasn't able to breath for himself. Four days later, Blessing came out of his coma and was healed completely. He didn't need oxygen at all, was walking around and was able to drive, and it seemed like everything returned to normal. We believed we had the victory over cancer and that was it.

One thing we were concerned about was that

Blessing had a girlfriend he wanted to marry for many years and was seeking permission to do so from her parents. In the meantime, we were debating whether it was God's will for him or not. We told him to make sure he prayed to hear from the Lord before he made a commitment to any woman. At this point, Blessing was a 29-year-old man, and had to make his own decision. He said it was the time for him to get married. They came to the house and we prayed, blessed and released them.

It was a big wedding because the invited and uninvited came to see this young man who was like the biblical character Lazarus who had been raised from the dead. Right after the wedding, however, the covering shifted from us, his family, to his wife. She never allowed us to pray for Blessing or administer any more alternative medication to him. A couple of months later, the cancer came back in full force. We advised Blessing to get back to alternative medicine treatments, but to no avail. That was the most painful part of that season of adversity.

My wife and I decided to go to Africa to refresh ourselves for about three weeks in November 2007. We could do this because I was self-employed and she was a consultant. We decided that after four years, it was enough time to go and take a break. We were in Nigeria when we received a call that Blessing had been rushed back to the hospital because the cancer had spread. We came back in December and in early 2008, it was time for us to resume morning, afternoon and evening shifts at the hospitals where the many treatments took place.

After a while, his body couldn't handle them anymore. During that time, we fought many battles with the hospitals, doctors, social workers, in-laws, and life itself. At the end, we no longer had much to offer Blessing. At some point, they declared him brain dead, because Blessing wasn't able to respond to anyone any longer after suffering a cardiac arrest. Maybe he was hearing us, but wasn't responding to our communication. The hospital refused to give him the normal treatment he deserved. And as bad as it was, it was in the very hospital where my wife worked, too. This made it difficult for her to handle.

At one point, the administration had told my wife to take a paid vacation for three weeks because she was influencing and interfering with the decisions the nurses and the doctors were making. We would go to visit, but Blessing would not be taken care of. Both of us joined efforts and rolled him around to clean him up, and it was painful to watch. One day they decided to take him to Shadyside Hospital. Then they disconnected him from his breathing machine after they met with his wife. We were not aware that was going to happen. The previous night, Blessing was awake, responding to us, and watching us as the family gathered around to pray for him.

The worst part of that was that his wife wasn't really a believer in Christ. Every time we would come to pray, she would leave the hospital room and would not join us to fight for Blessing's life. At some point, the wife and the family called the social worker of the hospital and in a hospital conference room declared Blessing dead, even though he was still alive. One morning on April 14, we got a call from the doctor that Blessing was no longer. We went into the hospital and saw Blessing lying there on his deathbed like a dead goat.

We had to make arrangements to bury our first born. It was a massive funeral with about 300 people in attendance. I was shocked to see some of the people who were there uninvited. I thank God for the African Christian Fellowship (ACF) family who surrounded us with great love. We offered our son to God, and believed God would comfort us, which He did.

After the burial, as we came back in the limousine, Blessing's wife apologized to us in her own way about whatever happened. That was the end of Blessing and the last we saw of his wife up to this writing. This was obviously a painful experience, and we have great compassion for any family that goes through the loss of a child.

Gary Mitrik, our pastor at Greater Works Outreach Church, played an important role in taking care of Blessing's final days, including requesting that people in the church give blood, and praying and fasting for him. Blessing was the second or third person I knew of who had his corpse brought into the church sanctuary for the funeral. The church fixed food and fed everyone who came to the funeral. The banks around Pittsburgh and Camp Kon-O-Kwee all played an important role in raising money for his burial. We buried him and came home and just spent time together as a family, the five of us, trying to move on with our lives.

We asked ourselves what we could do with this tragedy to make some sense out of it. I had a non-profit organization that I wanted to make a part of my overall business plan, and it already had an IRS approval. We decided on the date of his burial to petition to establish a family foundation in his name called The Blessing Foundation.

Our son Blessing loved children and poor people. After he became a teacher, I remember two incidents where he had done something that deeply touched me. One time I went to his room and saw papers all over the floor. I asked him about the mess, and he said those were all the names of his children in school. He was taking a count of them and reviewing their work to see where they stood and what he could do to help them in class.

The other time was when he told us he could feel the pain we felt as his parents when we sent him to school and he wasn't doing well. He wanted us to know that teachers were even in more pain when they saw that children were not doing very well in class. He loved children so much, and this is why the Foundation was established – to take care of the poor, orphans and those who cannot take care of themselves. Blessing was very much liked every-where he went.

Blessing's death was obviously a blow for all of us. I had to remain strong for my wife, even though I am still feeling the pain of the loss. Blessing and his mom were quite close, as was our daughter Peace who was deeply impacted as well. Even up to today, it is still a big issue in our lives. We seem to be coping with it better today, but it has left a void in our family that only God has helped us to fill as we go.

There are three major areas of emphasis for The Blessing Foundation. One program we are actively performing now is taking orphans and putting them through school, from the elementary up to the university levels. So far, we have been able to train three university students. One is finishing up in 2016 as a medical doctor and a surgeon in Uganda, and another is in public administration. Another graduated in social science in 2007. The second thing is to help out the widows through a program we call the Widow's Mite. The third thing we will do as money comes in is to provide a reliable water supply for remote villages. Water is a major problem in Africa and it gives us great joy to think that we can help children drink water in memory of our son.

I will never forget 2009 when I went to a place called Malara, Uganda, with ACF. There was a serious drought in this village. Only God knows why one place would have rain and another place not too far away had no rain for four months. The leader in the village took me to a place near his house and said to come and see where people get their water. I went to a little pit and there was no water in it at all, and what was there was muddy and dirty floodwater.

This program is so close to my heart because when I was a child, there were times when I ate dust and drank dirty water. I would grab sand, put it in my mouth when I was a small boy, mixed it with water and washed my body with it. As I said previously, that's why they gave me the nickname "Sand." If you looked at me then covered in sand dust and mud, you wouldn't be able to tell who I was. Water is one of the top program priorities for The Blessing Foundation as the Lord provides the money. The last emphasis for the Foundation is to provide initial capital for business startups.

I have told you about Blessing and have alluded to my other children by name, but I will devote the next chapter to telling you more about the family whom I love so much.

Chapter Ten
My Family

My wife and I have six children, four boys and two girls. The Lord first blessed us with Blessing, then Victor, Joy and Peace. Later on, Samuel and Emmanuel, Jr. joined our family through adoption in 2009 and 2010. Three of our children were born in Fort Wayne, Indiana. Blessing was born in Huntington where my wife and I arrived when we first came to America. We moved to Fort Wayne for a feel of urban life because Huntington was then merely a university village of a few thousand people. That made us feel lonely because we were immigrants accustomed to more a lively and busy African social life.

We moved to Pittsburgh, Pennsylvania in 1987 so my wife could attend medical school at the University of Pittsburgh. My children were still young then. They were busy with school and I was busy with work. I lived in the office and in the air travelling as an auditor, and never really had much closeness with my children. Mom spent every extra minute she had while in medical school to ensure our children were well cared for, and she had her mom around who helped immensely in raising the children.

One thing was certain in my family, and that was we rarely missed family devotions. We were always at the church on Sundays and during mid-week services. In fact, my children looked forward to being at church at all times because that was our social life and our source of strength. I felt like I committed a crime any day I did not take my children to church. Also, going to church was to me a source of rejuvenation after being on the road for a whole week and knowing that most of the times I would soon be heading to the airport for another trip.

If I was in town during the week, my children would always call me at work to remind me to come home early so they could go to midweek services. If I failed to take them, the evening would be like "To your tents O Israel," which is a way of saying they were not happy and I needed to minimize contact with them. I did not really know the technique of reassurance then.

Of course, our family devotions would always bring us to our knees and helped us to heal. We knew how to pray as a family and sometimes confessed our faults to one another. We learned how to make Jesus the center of our lives, the anchor of the family, and a shelter in the time of storm. Occasionally, we traveled together to visit friends and attend religious conventions, especially ACF conferences, and this helped us bond together.

Even though we had a busy life, I managed to take time out when I was in town to attend parent conferences at the children's school. This was important to me because I wanted to make sure they were doing well in school. I regret not being available to attend more of my children's school activities, such as sports and music. When I was able to attend, I was excited and my children loved my presence.

I encourage parents to avoid making the mistake I made of missing their children's young lives. This affected my relationship with my children, along with the fact that I was a tough disciplinarian. I realized later in their lives that I had to make amends and ask for forgiveness from each child. Today, I am closer to my children than earlier in their lives, and their regular homecoming, sometimes with friends and family, rejoices my heart. After they left home, we have converged and taken family trips as adults together, and frequently have quality family time, especially during holiday seasons.

I would also confess, like Jacob of old, that my family was a bit dysfunctional for many years because, to my shame, I argued frequently with my wife, especially when it came to disciplining the children. As both my wife and I matured, we came to realize that life is more enjoyable where peace and unity dwell. In spite of all I have said, I dearly love every member of my household, and thank God each day for giving me such a lovely wife and children. I am tremendously blessed to have them in my life. Honestly, they treat me well and love me dearly, and I love them, too. This is the Lord's doing.

Each of our children has a unique character given to them by God. Blessing was a good and friendly man who loved to have fun. To him, life was meant to be enjoyed, and that is true to some extent. He was highly athletic and won the MVP award as a basketball player in high school. He was a good player who loved to score from a distance, being quite accurate as a three-point shooter. He also received an Eagle Award, which is an award usually given to the student of the year at Greater Works Christian Academy. Blessing loved children and worked with the YMCA where he earned the title "Uncle Ike" at YMCA Camp Kon-O-kwee.

There at the camp, he was given the responsibility to recruit students from abroad. This gave him the opportunity to visit some cities in Europe. At one point, he brought seventeen students from London to sleep over one weekend in my house. I had fun interacting with these young folks. Because of his love for children, he decided to be a teacher specializing in elementary education with emphasis on special ed. During his illness, he was always mindful of others and handled the difficulties with little complaining. When he died, his funeral was attended by many people who came from all across the United States. Blessing has gone home to be with the Lord and we miss him dearly.

Victor was a determined and disciplined young man who was a leader in high school. Growing up, he knew when to stay away from television to get homework done without his parents scolding him to do so. It was easy for Victor to obey instructions, even when I was wrong. He was always bold enough, however, to speak out his mind in most situations. I know him as a straightforward man, and he did well in school. His positive behaviors shocked his friends who today still testify of his disciplined lifestyle that caused him to refuse to join in anything that would bring his family shame. He was a leader in college that earned him a four-year internship with General Electric Company, which right after graduation turned into a full-time job with the company.

Joy was born to be a mother. I watched her learn how to cook and do family chores that earned her the title "Mini Mom" from her siblings. She is still that way today and never really wanted any trouble from anyone. She copied well from her mom and derives great pleasure in serving others. Joy majored in communication in college and wanted to be a news anchor lady. She is a talented speaker and writer, while at the same time a naturally-gifted musician. After working with a publishing company for many years, she discovered she derives the most joy and satisfaction as a musician. As a singer, song writer and pianist, she is now touching many lives with her songs across the globe. She uses this platform to witness for Christ.

My daughter Peace is a natural leader. She is a strong and determined young lady and learned well from Daddy. She is very outspoken, and while growing up, her boldness conflicted often with Daddy's character and earned her some discipline. She always ran to Grandma for refuge from Daddy. Peace's strength has equipped her well to overcome adversities. She is a woman of faith and of excellent character, and tells you the way she sees things without fear.

As I look at her, I see a pillar poised to be

used for God's Kingdom in many ways. Peace has a scientific mind which led her to major in physical therapy and later earn a doctoral degree in that field. Peace is talented in counseling and is not intimidated in confronting and solving problems. She is a pianist, drummer, singer and songwriter, and is featured alone and sometimes with her sister on the stage.

Joy and Peace are great worship leaders. From their youth, they have always worked together and found great satisfaction in leading people closer to God through music in many Christian gatherings and events. Both have great compassionate hearts and have been on short-term mission trips to Haiti and South America.

I appreciate my children in many ways, especially their commitment to serve God without wavering, and I love them dearly. They are all well positioned to occupy till Jesus comes, fervent in spirit while serving the Lord. I am convinced that the hand of God is on my children, and they shall be mighty on earth as has been promised in His word. As it is written in Isaiah 8:18, "Here am I and the children the Lord has given me! We are for signs and wonders." It will not be by their efforts. The zeal of the Lord of hosts who dwells on Mount Zion will perform it and cause my children to pass the baton of faith down to their descendants.

As a family, we believe in the future God will enable us to establish elementary schools in Africa where we will be able to train and educate orphans. Instead of just sending money to help them out, the best thing to do would be to provide an educational environment where both the poor and rich can come to receive formal and spiritual education. Because of that commitment, we prayed and decided to pursue adopting several orphans to expand our family here in the United States and in Africa.

Samuel and Emmanuel, Jr, arrived in the United States in 2011. I discovered when they arrived that it's not a joke to raise children when you are in your sixties, especially doing the school work. One of them, Samuel, has an iron knee. We buy him jeans today, tomorrow they are all worn out with holes around the knee area. Shopping for clothes, helping with their homework, and shopping for school requirements are fun and challenging. We enrolled them in a Christian school sponsored by our church to help give them godly heritage. My wife is blessed to have them around, and I am, too. They are joyful children and the house is now full of joyful noise, especially when their sisters come to visit them. There is laughter everywhere.

For our two daughters, Joy and Peace, having the boys is like a dream come true. They are old enough to have their own family, and they treat the boys as if they are their own children. If they had the time, they would probably try to steal them away from us. Our prayer is that we will give the boys godly training that adds value to their lives so they will grow to be God-fearing and provide good value to our society.

There you have a little about my family members. I have referred to the African Christian Fellowship throughout this book. Let me now explain a little about this organization that has played such an important part in my family's life and history.

Chapter Eleven
Working with ACF

The African Christian Fellowship (ACF) is a dynamic organization. It was founded in 1977 as African Students Christian Fellowship. At first, it was composed of all students, a majority of whom were Nigerians. Shortly after the Nigerian-Biafran War, many Nigerians migrated to Europe, America and other parts of the world in pursuit of education and for survival. The schools in Nigeria could not provide space for the people who wanted to get educated, including me – especially those who didn't have money or Abraham as their father, as we like to say. As a result, there was a mass exodus of people who wanted to get a good education, especially to America because of the work-study program there. Some went to London and, over the years, the British have accepted more Nigerians than any other country. America also opened its arms to Nigerians and we flooded the land of opportunity in the early '70s and beyond.

Many Nigerian Christians were strong believers before the war, during the war, and after the war. But when they came over to the States, some of them embraced American life and began to lose their faith. There was nothing that would come close to the togetherness and community that we had while we were in Africa.

In the mid 70s, Billy Graham challenged people during a Campus Crusade conference to go and find their mission field. The African Christian students who were at that conference were fired up to do something. They wanted to form an organization that would both help themselves here in the States and also be able to go back to Africa someday to evangelize their homelands. Therefore, they founded the African Students Christian Fellowship. At the time, however, they were all students with little in the way of resources, trying to find a way out of school toward a career.

As time went on, many of them graduated and began to scatter, this time within America. To combat this, members decided to change the name of the organization and remove the word "students" that was part of their name. Washington D.C. was the first chapter to be registered and it now has a building that we use as our headquarters. Many of the ACF members are in Los Angeles, Louisiana, Houston and other cities, and some have their own facilities. We now have about 52 Chapters across the United States.

The new name after the change was the African Christian Fellowship with a national board and an appointed chairman. ACF has four regions – East, West, Midwest, South – with each region having several chapters. The role of the chairman is to lead the people ensure orderliness, and promote the stability of the Fellowship. Every other year ACF would have a national conference, which is like a homecoming for the members. Other conferences are held periodically within the national and regional structures.

The Pittsburgh Chapter of ACF was inaugurated at Duquesne University in 1991. God used my wife and I to encourage other Africans in the city to start a chapter after a Nigerian man, a Ph. D. student at the University of Pittsburgh, died. The man had two sons and, of course, his wife was depressed after his death. We took the two boys and brought them to our home so that his wife could regain herself. After that incident, my wife and I contemplated what we should do to get Africans together in Pittsburgh on a regular basis so we could encourage one another and take care of situations like the one described with the Pitt student.

ACF has four main objectives as an organization, and these are: 1) reconnecting with the continent of Africa; 2) building bridges between members and ministry opportunities; 3) passing down the legacy; and 4) building the ACF family and community. We want to pass down the legacy of our African heritage to our children, and make sure they are connected to their roots so at least they have the awareness that their parents came from somewhere. The vision of ACF is to be a thriving Christian community that models integrity, excellence, and compassion to mobilize and empower Africans worldwide to impact their generation and Africa. This vision is alive in the heart of every true member of ACF.

The program to reconnect our members with Africa was dormant for some time. In the mid '90s, however, one of our Fellowship members by the name of Richard started a missions program called ACF Missions, Inc. This was supported by our members, some of whom joined him in his missions efforts. He resigned the leadership of mission work at some point and started his own missions organization. I was appointed ACF Missions Director after him in 2007. This missions effort was managed by the East Region of ACF, but the work we did encouraged the West, Midwest and the South Regions to join in the missions effort at some point. At present, ACF missions efforts are thriving across Africa with hospitals and schools being built, churches being planted, and small businesses being established for the poor.

Over the years, I have received prophetic messages that I was to go to the mission field in Africa and the Islands. Early in 2007, a minister came to our church and was walking around after ministering, saying there was someone the Lord has been talking to about going to the mission field. And indeed, God had been talking to me privately about this issue over the years. This person asked that whoever it was should come out so she could pray for him or her.

Everyone was quiet for several minutes and no one was coming forward. She kept on walking around to my side, looking around. When I got up, she said she knew it was me but didn't want to embarrass me. She started out talking about my son, Blessing, who was then sick, for this was before he passed away. I was thinking, "How did she know about my son's illness, and how could I leave his situation and travel out of the country?" She was telling me the Lord was saying to go and He would take care of my situation.

Then she began talking about the countries I was going to visit during my ministry, even naming them, with Uganda being one of the countries. At that point, I thought to myself "This is serious" and decided to heed God's call. I went to the missions field in Uganda with four people that very year, replacing the ACF East Region former Missions Director. When we arrived in Uganda, nothing seemed to be on a solid foundation there. Therefore, the first thing we needed to do to be official was to register our NGO there as ACF-Uganda, and then we made changes in our local leadership team in order to be sustainable. That was how we would establish our credibility, especially with the government.

We also did pastoral training, evangelistic work, visited the children we sponsored, and reclaimed our 14 acres of property that had been purchased by the former director. Our land deed was in a foreign language, so we consulted a lawyer, had the document translated into English, and re-registered the land. The rigor of this effort alone was sufficient to fill our two-week missions visit. It was during that visit when the Lord gave me a vision for building a medical clinic on our property to benefit many, instead of an orphanage planned by my predecessor in the two buildings under construction.

The following year we went to the mission field again and the first thing we did was to meet with the government officials, which we have established as our custom for any visit. We went to see the mayor of the city to let him know what our plans and official goals were. The mayor told us, actually shedding tears while speaking, that Uganda was all ours and that it was the first time he had seen Africans returning to take care of Africans.

As each of the four ACF regions in the U.S. identified their own mission work, it spread ACF's name and purpose all over Africa – in the Congo, the Republic of Benin, Burundi, and Sierra Leone, where a major medical clinic has been finished. We have one clinic completed in Kabarole district of Uganda and a new one is being built in Kumi, the eastern part of Uganda. We also continue to sponsor orphans at all levels of academia. We at ACF talk regularly about the future of missions and what we need to do to increase the reach of our work. We have graduated many university students, including a medical doctor sponsored by my family. Some other students have graduated from technical and nursing schools.

We have workers in those countries we support and who, in our absence, sometimes organize their own mission efforts and go without us. If we have money, we send it to them, and if not, they raise their own funds amongst themselves. Our missions purpose is not to give philanthropic help to others. We have used our resources to create outreach tools to preach the gospel. That is why we hold open crusades during each trip and many people have come to the Lord. We also provide pastor's training, along with counseling for orphans and those in need.

Another good thing that has developed over the recent years is our efforts in church planting, which is spearheaded by my successor, Festus Ukwuani. When we go to a country like Uganda or the Republic of Benin in west Africa, we recruit some missionary doctors and nurses to join us, because it is difficult to get doctors to go full time to the mission field from America. We buy all our medication in Africa, because it isn't easy to ship anything from here over to Africa. Sometimes the children of our missionaries join us during the missions trip. In 2014, fifteen teenagers and young adults joined us. It is beautiful to observe our program fulfill the objective of passing down our African legacy to our children during these trips. Even if our focus is medical missions, I won't go into the field without preaching. When I preach and see people respond to the gospel and come for healing and prayer, it blesses my soul and makes the missions work more rewarding.

No one can conduct missions empty handed and without money. Every time I would load my pockets with money, I found that I could give it all away in no time at all because the needs are so great. Over the years, I wondered what I could do to get the money to be able to do missions work. Some in my organization were not in agreement with me when I was missions director that we should do business philanthropy. When my missions directorship was over, that freed me to pursue this goal without having a conflict of interest with ACF's objectives. I determined the best thing to do first was to acquire some pieces of property and find out what the Lord wanted to do with them. Presently, I have acquired three acres of land in Uganda. I am open to hear from the Lord as to what He wants me to do with the properties. And I know He will continue to speak and guide my efforts.

As I write, I have resigned my CFO position at the Health Center in order to pursue my love and passion for work in Africa. I am trusting the Lord that He will give me many more opportunities to minister there, but I am also aware that I am a pilgrim here on Earth and must be making progress daily. In the next chapter, I will describe yet another rescue that the Lord used to impress upon me the truth of James 4:14: "Why, you do not even know what will happen tomorrow. What is your life? You are a mist that appears for a little while and then vanishes."

Chapter Twelve
My Head Injury

The Bible states in Psalms 34:19, "The righteous person may have many troubles, but the LORD delivers him from them all." These were the words of King David, who experienced many afflictions. In 2014, I was beginning to get excited about what the Lord was indicating He had for me to do. I was contemplating retiring from my full-time job to continue tent-making through my consulting work. The heart of this matter was to find some way to embrace the business call that the Lord was laying on my heart to establish small businesses in Africa in order to support my ministry and other missions efforts. The pilot countries for these small business efforts were Uganda and then Nigeria, as the Lord provided funds. In order to do this, I had to obtain a multiple-entry visa to Uganda so I could travel as often as the Lord directed.

On July 22, 2014, I put my documents together and traveled to Washington D.C. to visit the Ugandan Embassy. My interaction with Embassy officials was friendly, and they welcomed my ideas and, in a short time, granted me a multiple-entry visa. I came home excited on a beautiful, sunny day in July. My wife was at work and our children Samuel and Emmanuel Jr. were in day care. I had some time to do my yard work, from which I derive great pleasure. I got dressed in my yard-care clothes and brought my tools out with me. My desire was to edge the front of my house and trim the trees on my driveway so they could look decent while I was away to the mission field. I had already booked my flight and was ready to leave the following week.

I love to praise the Lord with joyful songs when I am working in my yard, and this occasion was no exception. I plugged in my edger, switched it on, and began whistling a song, keeping beat with my lips, tongue and mouth as usual. Usually before I start trimming the trees, I spray them to see in case any bees or hornets are hiding inside. I had some past experiences with hornets, however, that led me to believe I had nothing to worry about. My past encounters had been at night, however, when I boldly cut the branches around them, trapped them – one time my wife helping me – and put them in a trash bag after I saturated them with hornet spray.

Unfortunately, this time I forgot to check for their presence, and began to edge the first of six trees along my driveway. After I finished one side of the first tree, I continued on the right side. Instantly, a drove of hornets came after me like a stream of war planes in the air. This time it was daylight, and the sun was at its full strength, which energizes these poisonous and deadly insects. I did not think to run, and I was spitting at them while my edger was still running in my hands. I was swatting at them with the edger, assured that I could chase off a few hornets as in the past.

All of a sudden, one of them came at me with great speed and stung me inside my nose. Immediately I fell, and I flipped over and hit my head with great force as I crashed to the ground. I somehow managed to run into my house and slammed the door. My glasses had fallen off my face as I fell, and I feared something was wrong because my head hit really hard on the ground. I phoned my wife immediately to let her know what had happened. She inquired if I would like to go to the emergency room, but I declined, saying that I was all right.

I picked up my spare glasses and looked outside to watch hornets invade and fly through my yard for several hours. Later that afternoon, I snuck into my car and drove off to pick up my children from day care. When I returned, the hornets were almost back into their nest, but my face was swollen and my head was hurting.

I went to bed at night and had a good sleep. When I awoke, my face was red. I did not think anything of it and went to work. On my way to work, I was suffering from a severe headache. When I got to the medical center, Kate, one of the doctors, refused me entrance into my office and took the key away from me. She rushed me to the emergency room for a CT scan, took my car to my wife's office, and gave her the key to the car so that I could not drive. Just as I thought, however, the scan showed I had a bad head bruise, but there was no fracture. The doctor recommended a week off from work to rest and fully recover.

Rest and fully recover, when I had a ticket to go the mission field that I had purchased for $2,400? I was a wounded soldier, but I was still able to fight, or so I thought. The next week, I took off for Uganda, defying any instruction or recommendations to stay home. One of the reasons I wanted to go to Uganda so badly was that it was the grand opening of the ACF medical clinic that the Lord had given me the vision for ACF to build in Uganda.

The grand opening took place the first day I was in Uganda, and it was indeed a pleasure to see the clinic open and serving the people in the Kabarole District in Uganda. During the rest of the week, we went into the interior villages of Uganda to do open air crusades and pastoral training. As usual, I preached for two days and used Tylenol to comfort my pounding headache. As if that was not enough, I flew out to Nigeria at the end of week, where I spent eight days taking care of personal business.

Two days before my departure from Nigeria, I heard something snap in my head, loud enough to wake me up at about 3:00 AM. I called my wife for prayer, not knowing what exactly had happened. There and then, I started to complain to my wife that we had not accomplished enough for the kingdom of God. I asked her if God called either one of us home tonight, what could we say we had accomplished for Him on earth? My wife wondered why I was up so late at night in Nigeria and why I was talking like that. We prayed for about one hour and I went back to sleep.

I spent two more days in Nigeria, but in the back of my mind, I knew something wasn't right. I did not know that I had internal bleeding in my brain. I took off on an Air France flight heading to

Paris. When I got to Paris, however, I started shivering as if I was standing outside in January cold weather, even though it was August. Then I thought maybe I had contracted malaria.

I had a long five-hour layover in Paris, and I really wanted to get home to the U.S. When it was time to board the Delta Airlines flight, I was among the first nine people allowed to board because of my frequent flyer status. Once I settled on my seat, I requested a cup of coffee and a blanket. I put my jacket on, drank my cup of coffee, covered myself with a red Delta blanket, and fell off to sleep. While in the air, I missed most of meals offered during our eight-hour flight. We landed in the U. S. the next day on a Monday evening. On Tuesday, I had a board meeting at which I had to present financial statements to the board of the North Side Christian Health Center, where I worked. I got up and tried to go.

As I was driving down the road, my head was pounding as if someone was beating on my head with a sledge hammer. Immediately I called one of my pastor friends, Gerard Amoroso, and requested prayer. He prayed for me for almost thirty minutes as I drove down the highway. As he prayed, the headache subsided and I was able to carry out my duties at work that day with minimal problems. The next day, however, the pounding started again. I called my primary care physician to find out what was going on.

At this time, the world started looking different to me, the atmosphere was becoming dim, and the earth was spinning around me. My doctor's office booked an appointment to see me on Friday August 22, 2014, shortly after my 65th birthday on August 16. When I saw my doctor, Dr. Thomas Burk, he spent about an hour listening diligently to me, recording every symptom I talked about. I thought it a bit unusual for a doctor to spend so much time with a patient. At the end of my visit, he recommended an MRI and a visit to a trauma clinic.

I had visited Dr. Burk, the month before I traveled to the mission field, as was my custom. During that visit, we had joked about God's power to preserve me at my age without any major illness. When the results came back, he was shocked. The MRI showed blood spreading in my head, having found a way to get inside my brain. Thank God it was sorted out on time. I was kidnapped right there, or so it seemed, to go to a hospital emergency room, where they indicated I had to go in for head surgery. I replied, "What? Not on this head!" That was of no avail. They found me a hospital bed to spend the night so surgery could be performed the next day.

On August 24, my surgeon, Dr. Eric Altschuler, came to my hospital room and indicated I was to go in for surgery the next day. I refused to have the surgery, explaining that God would see me through, not realizing the magnitude of the bleeding inside my head. Dr. Altschuler wanted me to know that God created doctors. I responded that I knew that all too well because I lived with one.

He humbly left the hospital room with his team and never came back.

Fortunately, there was a resident Indian doctor, whose name I cannot remember, who came to my room five times. The fifth time he said to me, "Mr. Ike, I highly recommend you do the surgery because the dangers of not doing it are great." He pulled the MRI to my bedside to let me see exactly what was going on. God bless this doctor. He would make a great missionary. At this time also, my wife has been arranging with Dr. Altschuler for my surgery. The surgery was scheduled for August 27. This was about six months after my wife had survived an emergency appendectomy, so we were spending much time in the hospital.

That morning around 9:45, they rolled me into the surgery. I committed my life in the hands of God and was peaceful. After anesthesia, I was gone until I heard, "Mr. Ike, wake up. We are done." I tried to wake up, but everything was blurry. I had to close and open my eyes several time to see clearly. I remember telling no one in particular, "My head, oh my head hurts, my head hurts." I had a nine-inch incision at the back of my head to help drain the blood. Then the ordeal began.

I went from the recovery room to an eight-day hospital stay with a pipe and a tube on the center of my head to drain fluid and blood for several days. It was a bit scary, but I had a will to live and survive the surgery. The devil, however, had a different plan, which did not materialize because the Lord was with me throughout the incident. I had experienced yet another rescue.

On the morning they moved me from the recovery room to my regular hospital room, I had three dreams. In one dream, I was walking in a heavy rain looking for a place where I had been invited for a party, but was unable to find it. As I was walking, I stepped into a deep ditch full of water and was drowning. That startled me, and I woke up immediately.

In the next dream, I was invited to a crusade. After the crusade, two brothers invited me to come and eat before going home. As I was going with them, the place began to look strange, so I attempted to leave. As I began to walk, I was barefoot, and I stepped into a burning neighborhood that looked like a ghetto. The farther I went, the more the ground looked like a pile of smoldering leaves and wood. Looking ahead, it was dark, and I said to myself, "This is the wrong way," and began to head the opposite direction. Then I woke up again.

The third dream lasted for about an hour. In that dream, a strong tornado came after my house. It was as if my house was situated on the ocean front. I was immediately quickened in my spirit to fight the storm, saying, "In the name of Jesus, perish!" Each time I said that, the storm would split, part to the right and part to the left. Then it regrouped into a different shape, sometime like a bear, a lion or some other strange animal. Through it all, I kept shouting: "In the name of Jesus, perish!"

After some time, my wife came and joined me shouting the same. Later, I saw Jesus in a boat with a group that looked like His disciples. When He showed up, the storm immediately stopped and disappeared. Then He anchored the boat and sent two of his companions who were small in stature to come to me. When they arrived, I was bold to ask them, "Are you for us or are you with the trouble makers?" One of them told me that the Lord sent them to come and let me know, "He is in the storm that you should not be afraid." Immediately, I woke up and had great peace that I was going to be fine.

Eight days later, I was discharged, but then the difficulty of moving around began. I could not easily sit down or get up, neither could I stand up for long. For about three months, I could not lie down to sleep either. Although the tube inserted on top of my head was removed, my head continued to accumulate fluid, and it felt like I had a shower inside my head. That was the way the mixture of water with blood sounded inside my head when I tried to bend over.

It was also quite painful, but over time my body absorbed all the fluid. I had to mold pillows and bed sheets around me so I could sit to sleep. I was also on many pain medications. I was having severe spinal pain at night such that I thought I was becoming paralyzed. I kept claiming my healing and with faith and authority, resisting and rebuking the devil to be gone from my spine. A week later, I was able to go to church with my family with the stitches still on my head. I had every assurance at that time that I was healed.

My mind and my intellect remained intact

and alert. In fact, immediately after the surgery, I sent my daughter to my car to get something I forgot to bring with me before the surgery. I vividly described where I parked my car and how she could get there. The day I was discharged, I had climbed 20 steps with my physical therapist. I had the will to live because, just as I had said to my wife when I called her from Nigeria, we have a lot more yet to accomplish for the kingdom of God. The verse in Proverbs 18:4 says, "The spirit of a man will sustain him in sickness, but who can bear a broken spirit? I am alive and well today because God rescued me again from death, and sustained my spirit. Thank God for my wife and children who prayed and took good care of me; for the intercessory prayer group in my church, Greater Works Outreach, and for friends who constantly prayed for me.

Let me conclude this chapter by saying that our God is an awesome God, and I will never forget He holds my life in His hands. In every situation, He cannot ever fail. As the verse in Psalms 9:10 says, "And those who know Your name will put their trust in You; for You, Lord, have not forsaken those who seek You." I have stated that God has much more for me to do, so let's move on to describe what I believe is my calling that has become more and more clear each time God has rescued me.

Chapter Thirteen
My Calling

Over the years, I have always wanted to learn about anything that would benefit me in life. Because I was empowered and educated by God, I came to believe that I could learn anything, and that I also had the ability to teach others what I had learned. That desire led to my learning more about the Bible. In 2001, I decided to finally quench my thirst of attending Bible school. As a result, I registered at the Greater Works School of Ministry because the school had trained many who are in ministry around the world. I never wanted to be a pastor or go into ministry, but one thing I did know was that God's hand was on my life to do something special for Him.

Therefore, I registered for one class to learn more about the New Testament. Then after that class, I registered for another and then for another. This was a part-time study regimen because I had full-time employment along with my consulting firm that I managed. After seven years in school, I had enough credits to be ordained a minister of the Gospel, which took place in 2008. This was the year after I became the Director of Missions for the African Christian Fellowship (ACF) in 2007. It was then that I first noticed the joy I had when I was preaching and teaching.

The missions work for ACF was both challenging and enjoyable at the same time because it gave me an opportunity to reach out in practical ways to those who were suffering, and also provided me an opportunity to preach the Gospel of Jesus Christ. I found that as much as I was giving out, I was receiving so much more in return. My first trip to the mission field was a baptism by fire because there were only five people on our team and the needs were great. I had scheduled open air crusades, a pastor's training workshop, and business meetings with the local team in Uganda. It was like we were trying to run a church in another country in two weeks with only a few assistants.

The joy I felt while helping the people and leading them to Christ was overwhelming, so much so that in 2008, only three months after my son died, I traveled back to Uganda again. This time, my team from ACF was bigger, so we expanded our work to include a medical mission, and began to make arrangements to build the medical clinic.

During this trip, an insane man who had actually killed a lady in the village came to our medical outreach. This man followed me around everywhere I went, singing strange songs all the time. I was afraid, especially after I heard that he had killed someone. I went to the pastor of the church where we were conducting the medical outreach, and requested that the insane man be sent away. The pastor told me, however, that there was nowhere in the village to send him since we were in a remote town by the name of Kumi, Uganda.

I gathered up my courage and requested an opportunity to preach in the market place since it was a market day. I was concerned because the insane man still followed me everywhere I went. A loud speaker was set up and music was played before I actually spoke. As the music played, the insane man walked up and down singing his strange songs. I preached a message based on John 4 about the woman at the well who had an encounter with Jesus. At the end of my preaching, four people came to the Lord, and one of them was the insane man. He came toward me with such force that I backed up, thinking he was about to attack me. I regained my composure, however, and gave Bibles to the other three converts, ignoring the insane man who obviously had no intent to harm me. When the meeting was over, he had stopped singing those strange songs and did not follow me again.

In 2009, I went back to Uganda and traveled back to Kumi. When I arrived, I was told that the insane man was in his right mind. My reaction was: "What? I want to see for myself!" The leader of our team in the village, Peter Charles, found him and brought him to me. When he arrived, I saw that the man was completely healed. I hugged him and told him I wanted to hear what had happened to him. One thing stood out of all the story he told me and that was, "At the time the music was playing and when I came to the altar call, I knew I was healed."

This was not the end of the story, because when the villagers noted that he was healed, they sued the family and took all their land properties. He sent a message from Uganda for me to help his family reclaim their land. I did that, and then the

Lord directed me to put him in school, which I also did. Today, that man is a graduate from a school of masonry and is functioning normally. I earned the title "Daddy" after this experience, because I had adopted a spiritual son.

In 2010, I went back to Uganda, again to Kumi. This time there was a famine and it had not rained for four months in Malara, one of the villages 45 minutes away from Kumi. We went there to distribute food and what I saw caused my heart to ache. The ground was cracked and dry, ant mold was everywhere on the ground, farms were scorched from the heat of the sun, and the storm-water well they had dug for cooking and drinking was dried up.

The people in Malara had gathered together, waiting for us to arrive so they could get some food that we were bringing. When we arrived, the people gave out a shout as if a king had come. Of course, King Jesus was present because He ordered us to travel to the village. It made me think of the Bible verse that says, "How beautiful on the mountains are the feet of those who bring good news, who proclaim peace, who bring good tidings, who proclaim salvation, who say to Zion, 'Your God reigns!'" (Isaiah 52:7).

We had to take care of the most important business first. We preached the Gospel and prayed for them, and then we distributed the food we had brought. Right there the miracles began to happen. A pregnant woman, whose name was called to receive her portion of food, went into labor and gave birth to a baby boy. They gave the baby boy the name Emmanuel.

During our prayer time, we had specifically asked God to send rain to Malara. While we were praying, just like it happened in the days of Elijah, I saw a small cluster of clouds in the sky near the village. I called on God to move the clouds closer as the team members were praying in one accord for the people. Lo and behold, at 2:00 AM the next morning, it poured torrential rain with lightning and thunder that woke me up from my sleep in Kumi. I prayed again that God would send the rain to Malara, just like it was raining in Kumi. In the morning, the local team leader said his wife called at 2:00 AM and said it was raining cats and dogs in Malara. The next year in 2011, our team was told that Malara had their best harvest ever.

I am motivated to preach and teach the word of God because the truth that changes lives is contained in the Scriptures, but must be appropriated by faith. In the Word of God there is life, wisdom, and victory for all who live by it. When the Holy Spirit enlightens and empowers the preached word with anointed power and authority, it is like launching a missile that hits its target precisely.

I am still learning to be a more effective teacher as the Holy Spirit, my Teacher, opens my eyes to understand more of His word, something for which I hunger and thirst. I will continue to accept opportunities given me to preach and teach God's Word because I know that every utterance of His Word will not return to Him void, but shall accomplish what God pleases and shall prosper in the thing for which He sent it (see Isaiah 55:11). When I speak as God's representative, He takes His Word and does what He pleases with it, like He did with the insane man. I did not anticipate then that God's word could reach someone in his condition, but it did, and that reminded me of the power in His preached Word.

I don't only enjoy preaching and teaching the Bible, but also teaching others my professional accounting skills. Part of the work I do is to design accounting systems and train people in government churches, nonprofits and small business entities to use those systems that provide effective financial accountability. I also provide internal control advice that helps augment an accounting system to function more efficiently.

I use accounting software to accomplish these tasks, and then help structure policies and procedures that facilitate good recordkeeping, transaction recording, and compliance monitoring. Over the years, I have discovered there is a great need for this service around the world, and I have traveled across the United States and to other countries to provide these services to non-government organizations that have been awarded government and foundation grants and for churches that depend on membership contributions.

As I provide these services, I have learned that God is the greatest Accountant ever known, because He is so precise in His recordkeeping to the penny. As stated in Matthew 10:30, "But the very hairs of your head are all numbered." He also keeps records of every human deed great and small. I call these books "Eternal Subsidiary Ledgers" where all the activities of all of mankind are recorded.

Then there is another book, the Book of Life, which I refer to as The Balance Sheet, that is used to judge the dead according to their works (see Revelation 20:12). So you see, our God is a great Record Keeper, and He does it with absolute accuracy and precision. This challenges me to provide services for my clients to ensure that their record keeping is reliable, which hopefully will lead to an invitation to come back and do more work for them.

The passion to teach accounting has also led me to teach college students, for I remember how my life changed when I was able to sit for my education. For more than five years, I served as an adjunct professor of accounting at local community colleges in the Pittsburgh area, and at Geneva College at the Center for Urban Biblical Ministry campus. In one of my classes, a student asked why her previous professor was not able to explain the rudiments of accounting as she was able to hear and understand them from me.

I believe that every entity on earth, including families, should make every effort to learn and apply good accounting and money management principles. This includes an understanding of budgeting and savings strategies, because money has wings and flies away quickly if it is not properly managed (see Proverbs 23:5). As it is commonly said, there may come a rainy day during which poor monetary management will deprive the organization, family or individual, and even ministries, of needed resources.

My son Samuel was five years old when he said, "If you do not manage your money well, you may not have enough to buy an umbrella when the rainy day comes." He said this when I was teaching him the importance of savings and lacked the words to finish my thought. He took my teaching over and completed the lesson for me.

The essence of teaching people and organizations to understand and apply accounting focuses on accountability. At all levels of life, family, businesses, governments, churches and people require accountability. They want and need to know where the monies come from and where they are going. Historically, husbands and wives have argued over issues of accountability and money, and some of those disputes have led to divorce.

Businesses and nonprofits have closed, governments have gone bankrupt, and churches have shut their doors, forfeiting their purpose for existence, which was to save souls and disciple people for the kingdom of God. All that happened because there was no accountability or good record keeping. I take my calling to teach accounting and sound financial management seriously, and when the opportunity arises to educate others, I have always given it thoughtful consideration.

It is time to close this book, but before we do, I want to make some comments in the conclusion that will summarize what I hope you will take away from this reading. I have been rescued again and again, and writing this memoir has been a wonderful exercise for me, as I have taken time to reflect on my life. Let me leave you with some final thoughts and reflections as I conclude my story in this book.

From Nothing to Something

If I were to give this book another title, it would be *From Nothing to Something*. This is because God is the only one who could have made all the things you have just read possible in my life. He brought me up out of a horrible pit, out of the miry clay, set my feet upon a rock, and established my steps, as stated in Psalm 40:2. When I was prepared to be nothing and go nowhere, He looked at me and said, "Son, it is about time for you to draw near to me so I can make something beautiful out of your life."

This reminds me of the verse in James 4:8 that states "Draw near to me and I will draw near to you. Cleanse your hands you sinners; and purify your hearts, you double minded." Those words are God speaking to anyone who is willing to come close to Him. My life was turned around only when I opened my heart to God and allowed him to change me. Although things did not instantly change, all things actually became new from the beginning of my walk with Him. I was able to learn how to pray and read the Bible, and I have the joy of life that flows from God and God alone.

God taught me perseverance, and revealed the meaning of my name Emmanuel, which when interpreted is "God with us." From then on, I learned to talk with God through prayer and meditation on His Word. In the early days of my Christian walk, I would clearly hear a voice frequently calling me "My son." I knew it was God calling me to give me wise instruction because my mother and my father were not there to give me advice.

I had a burning commitment in me to know Him more because I found that true wisdom comes from God and Him alone. It says in Proverbs 3:5, "Trust in the Lord with all your heart, and lean not on your own understanding; in all your ways acknowledge Him, and He shall direct your paths. Do not be wise in your own eyes; fear the Lord and depart from evil." He has truly directed my path and showed me a better way, and He can do the same for anyone who is willing to listen to Him.

Before leaving Nigeria for the United States, I heard the voice of wisdom advising me to write down the things I desired and expected to happen in the next five years of my life. That included when to get married, when to have my first child, when to graduate from college and so on. I wrote those things down and forgot all about them until the day I graduated from college. While packing my luggage with my wife to move to Fort Wayne, Indiana in 1980, I found the list I made in 1976. As I read through it, I discovered that every item on the list happened on the date I desired. This is the Lord's doing and it is marvelous in our eyes. (see Psalm 118:23)

I still am in the habit of making a prayer request list today and, as God meets each need, I check it off and focus on another. Our needs will always be there, and we cannot force God to fulfill them. Only God can make things happen in our lives, but this requires that we constantly come to Him in fasting and prayers.

When God began working with me, many of my friends began coming to me for advice to find out how I managed to finish high school in three years at home while they had been at it for five years. This provided me an opportunity to introduce them to my God who had turned my life around. As young adults, this was not easy advice for many of them to hear. I lost many friends in the process, but gained many others who I carefully chose.

I was determined to succeed in life and was thrifty to save every penny that came into my hands. You have read how often I fasted and prayed, and how I loved to read my borrowed books. I hired tutors when necessary to get additional help and borrowed money from friends to pay those tutors. When I arrived in the United States and saw a great opportunity around me, the need to work harder and succeed in life burned in my heart.

I was alone and did not really have many friends before my wife joined me in the States. My greatest desire was to bring her over to the United States and that happened in 1977. This was a great victory because I needed her around to pray and plan with me. We worked hard together and were in school together, raising children at the same time. When I graduated from college in three-and-a-half years, I knew for real that hard work pays off.

After my graduation, there was the need to work and save money to finish my Masters program, raise my children, and give to my extended family. The story goes in Africa that when you become educated, you do not care for your immediate family only but you then become the savior of all your relatives, so to say. My wife and I did this to the max and sometimes overdid it.

Life actually became busy for us when we moved to Pittsburgh because I was now a corporate auditor and my wife was in medical school. Our marriage sustained a major setback at this time of our lives. My wife was also going through sleepless nights, which lasted for many years, but God sustained us by His grace and mercy. When my wife graduated from medical school, our children were grown and off to college.

At one point, we had four of them in the university. This was not easy but we pressed on. As we passed through the hurdle of having our first child graduate in 2003, cancer attacked our first son and ended up taking his life in 2008. Life truly became tough to bear and a chilly gloom descended on the family at this time. God proved Himself faithful once again, and stepped in with His strength and comfort to sustain us and heal that devastating wound.

As our children graduated from college, became employed, and moved on with their lives, the empty-nest syndrome set in, providing a new challenge we had never faced. In 2014, as we were recovering from the death of our son, my wife and I each had a major surgery, resulting from a ruptured appendix in my wife's case and my fall that required surgery and left a nine-inch scar on my skull. With God's miraculous help, we pulled through, and these surgeries are now healed with no ongoing affects in our lives. God wanted us to be present for our children and grandchildren as they go through their own life to encourage them.

I hope you realize, my friend, that the way to life is not always fair. David wrote in Psalms 34:19, "Many are the afflictions of the righteous, but the Lord delivers him out of them all." This is my testimony, for I have learned that God always rescues His own as He promised. In the process, however, your perseverance and faith in Him are necessary to pull through, and sometimes you only emerge victorious through prayer and fasting (see Matthew 17:21).

This book has described being rescued from one thing and another and I have always seen God keep His promises. He is indeed a faithful God. I am truly convinced that He has rescued me from these predicaments to fortify and empower me and give me the opportunity to rescue others as He directs. I know that God uses people to rescue other people unless He chooses to do it all by Himself.

My family and I just finished celebrating a Christmas holiday when all the family was together, including Zoe, our first grandbaby. We had a wonderful time together, and we thank God that He is expanding our family, making the loss of Blessing a little less painful as we see the hope and future represented by our growing family.

As I finish, I am back in Africa where I received an update on the brother described in Chapter Ten who was delivered for his mental affliction. It is profound because God rescued me, and then used me to rescue that man, whose name is David. Here is the report I got:

David is fine and has come back home from Kampala, Uganda where he was working. He graduated in 2013 with skills in brick laying and concrete practice. I was with him yesterday and he sends his heartfelt greetings. He says he has missed seeing you. The Lord has done much in his life, restoring him to a sound mind. His testimony affects many people's lives here in Kumi. We are proud of his life and happy at what the Lord has done whenever we remember him.

God has rescued me so many times because He has had a purpose for my life. He has a purpose for your life, too. I have told my story to encourage you to have faith in God. If I was able with His help to do what I have done, then I know you will also be able to do great things for Him. There were times when I thought I would not make it, but here I am, still serving the Lord. I am confident in the Lord and optimistic about the future, and I trust that this book is my first among many. Thank you for reading, and to God be the glory!

Emmanuel N. Ike, CPA, CFE

Emmanuel N. Ike is a Certified Public Accountant and a Certified Fraud Examiner. He has served as the Chief Financial Officer at North Side Christian Health Center, a medical clinic located in Pittsburgh Pennsylvania funded by the US federal government and foundations. He is the President of Precept Consulting, Inc., a financial consulting firm based in Pittsburgh, Pennsylvania. Mr. Ike graduated from Huntington University in Huntington, Indiana with a B.S. in Accounting and Business Administration, and obtained his Master's Degree in Accounting and Financial Information Systems from Cleveland State University. Mr. Ike has more than 31 years of experience in accounting, auditing, fraud investigation, and investment placement for businesses and individuals, including Fortune 500, mid-size and small companies. He was a partner in a public accounting firm where he served as the Vice President Consulting for four years. He was also an adjunct professor of accounting at Geneva College at the Center for Urban Biblical Ministry and local community colleges. Currently, his consulting firm specializes in installing, designing and customizing accounting systems, internal control structuring, training, budgeting, investment placement, and tax planning for high income individuals, small businesses and non-profit organizations.

Mr. Ike has served with the African Christian Fellowship since 1991 in various capacities, including a position on the national board, missions director, treasurer and chapter president. Today Mr. Ike is the Executive Director of a nonprofit organization called The Blessing Foundation, established in memory of Mr. Ike's son who lost his life to cancer at age 29. The Blessing Foundation is a family foundation that has created programs in East Africa and Nigeria that include medical care, educational assistance, and economic development.

Mr. Ike has served on the board of directors for numerous non-profit organizations. He is happily married and has five children, and serves the Lord Jesus Christ with passion and sincerity of purpose, especially in the mission field.

Contact Information

You can contact Emmanuel Ike for more information on his work in Africa or to secure his consulting services through the following means:

412.260.9008 (USA)

412.573.9009 (gmail)

+234-909-362-5176 (Nigeria)

ike@askprecept.com

enikecpa@gmail.com

You can also learn more about
The Blessing Foundation at its website:

www.theblessingfoundation.org

ike@theblessingfoundation.org

Tax-deductible contributions can be made to
The Blessing Foundation through PayPal or
by sending a check to:

The Blessing Foundation
P. O. Box 230
Murrysville, PA 15668

You can also find Emmanuel Ike on Facebook,
Twitter and LinkedIn.